THE MAG

MYSTERY

 a beginner's guide

TERESA MOOREY

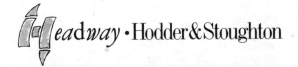
Headway · Hodder & Stoughton

For Frith Wood in Bussage,
Gloucestershire, and all other woodlands

Acknowledgements
Special thanks to Chel Bardell, of the Ozzie Pagan Alliance, and to Sandi
Leir-Shuffrey, for providing information for this book.

By the same author, in this series
The Moon and You
Witchcraft
Paganism
Herbs for Magic and Ritual
Shamanism
The Goddess
Earth Mysteries
Pagan Gods for Today's Man with Howard Moorey

Also
The Wheel of the Year – Myth and Magic Through the Seasons with
Jane Brideson

Order queries: please contact Bookpoint Ltd, 39 Milton Park, Abingdon, Oxon
OX14 4TD. Telephone: (44) 01235 400414, Fax: (44) 01235 400454. Lines are open
9.00–6.00, Monday to Saturday, with a 24 hour message answering service. Email
address: orders@bookpoint.co.uk

A catalogue record for this title is available from The British Library

ISBN 0 340 70494 2

First published 1998
Impression number   10 9 8 7 6 5 4 3 2 1
Year   2003 2002 2001 2000 1999 1998

Copyright © 1998 Teresa Moorey

Typeset by Transet Limited, Coventry, England.
Printed in Great Britain for Hodder & Stoughton Educational, a division of Hodder
Headline plc, 338 Euston Road, London NW1 3BH by Cox and Wyman Limited,
Reading, Berks.

CONTENTS

I think that I shall never see
A poem lovely as a tree ...

Poems are made by fools like me
But only God can make a tree

Joyce Kilmer, *Trees*

Much verse has been created to the glory and beauty of trees. Trees inspire art and music and evoke a sense of reverence, peace and awe. They connect us with the passage of the seasons and the enduring mystery of life, and their world has always been an integral part of ours. They provide us with wood for fires, furniture, boats, doors and beams. They are the lungs of our planet, breathing out oxygen into the atmosphere. Trees yield medicines, host abundant wildlife, underpin many legends and suggest enchantment and mystery. As their branches spread in layers, from close to the ground to high up in the embrace of the winds, so trees are an intrinsic part of our lives at all levels, from basic practicality to the most exalted forms of spirituality.

Deforestation and the wanton destruction of trees is part of our present problem and it is no coincidence that the occurrence of crime is higher in the inner cities, where few trees grow, to nourish and balance the soul. The ancient Celts believed that trees housed the spirits of their tribal ancestors or gods and goddesses – as they communed with trees so they were connected to wellsprings of strength and wisdom that were their birthright. Trees were planted upon burial mounds so that the spirit of the departed could live on within the form of the tree, existing as one with the tree 'essence'. People will risk life and limb to save trees from being chopped down and, even if our ideas about how such notions arose are hazy, many trees are held as sacred or special. Trees are hugged for their healing powers and people drawn to the mysteries of nature seek to make contact with them, even though the enchantment of trees can never, quite, be encapsulated.

Growing up in a small town in Somerset, I took the proximity of the countryside for granted. Like many children I wove stories and dreams in secret spots where nothing could be heard but the friendly giggle of a small stream and the low drone of insects. Usually my back was against a tree. That sense of being protected, embraced and connected was something I also took for granted, feeling that trees were my friends. I vividly remember a poignant moment, when I was eighteen and travelling to Bristol. My bus stopped outside a garden where two men were attempting to fell a tree, a more brutal and thoughtless process I have yet to see. It was summer and the sap was in full flow – I believe the tree was an apple tree. The men's tools obviously inadequate to the task, they were using a mixture of chopping and yanking at limbs, to bring low this beautiful creature. Its branches grabbed in agony at the blue sky and it kept trying to pull itself back up to the erect position it had no doubt held for many years. I burst into tears, to the embarrassment of my companion. Everyone else on the bus discretely ignored me – and the calls of the tree, which no one else seemed to hear. Our sense of the life in trees and the general sanctity of nature is a sense we seem

to have lost – and unlike a blind person whose hearing sharpens to compensate, no such inner balancing has taken place in the human heart which now coldly exploits and wastes many of the gifts of the earth.

It seems to me impossible not to commune with trees, for their soft, meditative chanting is heard clearly by the soul. More specifically, they are laden with symbolism and magical significance, possess many links with ritual and pagan worship and have extensive mythology attached to them. In the following pages we shall be exploring themes such as: the Tree of Life, the meanings of the Yule Log and other traditions, the linkage of trees with the thirteen moons of the year and the Celtic Ogham alphabet. The significance of trees in shamanic cosmology will be examined, along with charms and folk customs.

From the Buddha to Isaac Newton many people have found revelation in the presence of trees. Could it be that in some way we can't quite express that trees form the entrance to another dimension, consciousness or state of being? Something within us seems to say that trees are more than they appear and are greater than the sum of roots, trunk and branches. If you are a lover of trees – if you sense their fascination, and would like to explore their esoteric message, or simply intensify your appreciation and enjoyment, I hope you will find information in these pages interest and fire your imagination.

Teresa Moorey, Samhain, 1997

N.B. Information concerning medical remedies given in these pages is for interest and general knowledge. Other works should be consulted for specific recipes and uses. **Take great care**. Some trees are very poisonous and you must ensure that you identify species correctly.

folk customs and symbology

For we are up as soon as any day-o,
And for to fetch the summer home
The summer and the May-o
For summer now has come

'Hal-an-tow', Helston Furry Dance Song

Folk customs possess a fascination. We feel they must be telling us something about our roots and our history and we wonder about their true significance? Do they contain secrets, a hint of a wisdom we have lost? Or are they just about good times and celebrations?

Many folk customs are connected with trees, their lore and symbology. The link between humans and trees is instinctual – trees stand erect in a way similar to ourselves. In fact, the Native Americans call them the 'standing people'. However, our lives are

more fleeting and while we may move about on the surface of the earth, the roots of the trees penetrate deep within it and their branches reach high up towards the sky. Their lifespans being much longer than ours – in some cases hundreds or thousands of years – we feel their profound connection with the passage of the seasons, the ages and all the many changes that affect the earth. Our knowledge being so comparatively superficial, trees are our memory.

The forest has been considered as embodying the mysteries of the Feminine and as such a place of initiation. However, a forest may also be a place in which we get lost, 'unable to see the wood for the trees' – the forest can enlighten or mean lack of spiritual awareness. For the Australian Aborigines the forest signifies the Beyond, a realm of spirits and deep experience. From the Babes in the Wood to the legends of King Arthur, the forest is where strange and transforming events take place. Shrines to Aphrodite were places in wild, inaccessible places, such as the tangled heart of the forest, to mark the awesome nature of her power.

All parts of the tree have different meanings. In the old Chinese elemental system wood, along with metal, water, fire and earth, comprise the five elements. Wood correlates with the east and with wind, and may be associated with spring and the colours blue and green. Used to make cradle and coffin, table, chair, bed, gallows, ship and door, wood is the shaper and container of life. Each tree is, in a sense, a 'doorway' to another dimension. Nuts and seeds obviously signify fertility and potential – a secret, dormant, receptacle of life to come. Fruit is a culmination, a reward, a sacrifice and a transition. Leaves tell of the seasonal changes, green for resurgence and hope, brown for mourning and departure. Resin is considered to be the soul of the tree. Amber is the fossilised resin of cone-bearing trees and is one of the oldest materials used for human adornment. Because it is warm to the touch it was thought to contain life. Jet, which is fossilised wood, is a 'magical mate' to amber. Both become electrically charged when rubbed. Some priestesses wear necklaces of alternating amber and jet because they are considered to represent, respectively, projective and receptive forces. They are composed of primordial tree-essence, far older than our humanity can comprehend and yet speaking to us of primal life.

There are specific customs and stories associated with almost every individual species of tree and many customs linked to trees in general. The whole tree symbolises the totality of creation, from the depth of the earth to the starry crown of the sky encapsulating each phase of existence, from birth through growth, mating, fertility and decomposition. A tree is a promise of continuity and eternal life – hence the term 'Tree of Life' which has many meanings, some of which we shall be discussing later.

The Green Man

The Green Man, rendered by medieval masons on many churches, is a fairly recent creation historically. He is the foliate mask – a face made up with foliage growing from his mouth, around his eyes and

from his nose. He is the embodiment of the nature spirit, the living pulse of the tree as it is felt by our humanity. It may be that the Green Man is a pagan reference incorporated into Christian architecture and is worth looking out for in church engravings.

The Green Man is truly an image of immeasurable antiquity as is the original Wild Man, the flagrantly erotic and untamed heart of the forest and a storehouse of primal power. He is rather more than a leafy embodiment of nature's bounty! He has links with all aspects of the Nature Spirit, such as the Corn King – the Spirit of the Corn, who is a pagan aspect of the God who gives his life each year in the harvest, to be born anew the following spring.

The Green Man is present in the guise of folk heroes such as Robin Hood. The yearly sacrifice of the Corn Spirit was paralleled in many ancient religions by the sacrifice of an actual king. This apparently happened in England as recently as 1100CE, when King William Rufus was shot by an arrow, in the New Forest, seemingly at his own wish. This event, tellingly, took place during the festival of Lammas at the end of July and is, traditionally, the time for the death of the Corn King. While this was a literal death – and we may be sure that plenty of human sacrifice was practised in times gone by – the true meaning is that the God undergoes an underworld passage and initiation. He becomes King of the Shadowlands until the time comes for him to re-emerge, at the Winter Solstice, with the rebirth of the sun. So it is that the ideas of death, resurrection and enlightenment are connected with trees and specifically with hanging upon a tree. Christ hung upon the Cross. Odin hung upon the World Tree, Yggdrasil, until he gained knowledge of the Runes in a shamanic revelation. The coffin of Osiris, when he became king of the Egyptian Land of the Dead, was deposited within a tree.

Oak King and Holly King

Initiation and underworld journey transform our idea of the Nature God from the joyful spirit of the greening vegetation to a powerful hidden presence. This was embodied as two aspects of the God, known as the Holly King and the Oak King, who battled twice a year at the Solstices, for ascendancy and the favour of the Goddess. Holly King, as King of the Waning Year, always wins at Midsummer as the sun goes into imperceptible but undeniable decline. Oak King, as King of the Waxing Year, wins at Yule, the Midwinter Solstice and presides over the time when the sun achieves 'rebirth' and grows in strength. These are the Dark God and the Light God. Neither is 'better' for both portray elements that are equally necessary.

The drama of Oak King and Holly King underlines many other stories, such as that of Gawain and the Green Knight in Arthurian legend. The Green Knight is a spirit who must be slain, who begs to be slain and yet can never be truly done away with. Oak King and Holly King are truly the twin guardians of the year. Oak is widely revered as a royal tree, with oracular powers, drawing to itself the lightning flash and yet surviving. Both holly and oak were especially sacred to the Druids – holly with its evergreen leaves and bright berries symbolised everlasting life and vitality.

The Christmas Tree

Most homes boast a brightly decorated tree, whether real or artificial, at Christmas. How many of us, however, have any idea what this tree actually signifies?

All forms of evergreen are held sacred to the Goddess, for evergreens do not shed their leaves and die. Thus the evergreen stands for She who is always with us and while Her countenance may change through the seasons, She is not usually visualised as departing to the Underworld, as the God does. While the God is introduced to the mysteries and travels the yearly cycle, the Goddess *is* the mystery and the cycle. Of course many trees are sacred to Her, but at Christmas, the evergreen is symbolic of continuing life, often topped with a fairy – a trivialised but pretty goddess-figure.

The Christmas tree is decorated with bright colours to coax the return of the sun at the Winter Solstice – for Christmas is the old pagan festival of Yule, when the God was seen as born anew of the Goddess. The yearly cycle can be interpreted as the 'love story' of

Goddess and God. The God, born at Yule, grows to young manhood in the Greenwood until He is ready to take his place as the consort of the Goddess. This is usually celebrated at the festival of Beltane, at the beginning of May. As the year progresses He matures until, as we have seen, He is cut down with the corn at Lammas, at the end of July, from whence he dwells in the Underworld until He is reborn again, son of His own fathering. This story represents the cycle of life and has nothing to do with incest. The traditional festivals marking this cycle, of which there are eight, are explored fully in *The Wheel of the Year – Myth and Magic Through the Seasons* (see Further Reading).

The Christmas Tree was introduced to Britain by Prince Albert, husband of Queen Victoria and developed from, originally pagan, German Yuletide celebrations. The Christmas tree tradition probably evolved from the Druidic custom of decorating groves of pine trees with lights and bright objects at Yule. Thus the light of the Divine is represented by a shining tree. Pines and fir trees are often associated with birth – these are trees chosen by storks for their nests and we all know the story of the stork bringing the baby. Here these evergreens are connected with the birth of the sun-god. The concept of the Christmas tree may have evolved from a much earlier tradition of 'moon trees' where a tree, or a pillar, topped with a crescent moon was covered with fruit and lights as a celebration of the sky-goddess. In the depth of winter, when branches are bare and moonlight glitters on frost-spangled tree-crowns, we are reminded of the life that endures when all is barren – the inner light of the soul.

These days it is far more environmentally conscious to use a small living tree, which we can plant outside later, or decorate a fallen bough or artificial tree, for the symbolism remains the same.

The YuLe LoG

Most often seen nowadays as a table decoration – or made of chocolate! – the Yule Log was, in times of yore, a substitute for the ritual bonfire that was lit at Hallowe'en (also called Samhain, pronounced *saween*) and Beltane. Jacqueline Memory Paterson (see Further Reading) tells us that 'In Europe druids burned great fires of pine at the Winter Solstice to draw back the sun and this practice became the custom of burning the Yule Log'. There are various traditions attached to this log – some say it should be oak, some say ash, others birch. A piece of the Yule Log should be kept to kindle the following year and ensure continuing life, luck and love.

The Druids

A likely meaning of 'druid' is 'wise man of oak' but, like most pagan traditions, the true origin of druidry is unclear. Druids have been connected with sinister practices, as have other pagan paths, although they have generally been associated with the wise and inscrutable. Druidry is intimately linked to trees, for these were considered a shamanic doorway to knowledge of Otherworld. The three grades of the druid – the bard, the ovate and the druid her/himself are each associated to a specified tree. The Bardic grade enshrines the powers of sound and memory, when the initiate learns hundreds of scripts by heart and keeps alive the knowledge of the generations – this is represented by the birch tree. The Ovate grade, of the prophet, seer and diviner, is linked to the yew tree, and opens the doors of time. The final grade is that of the Druid her or himself, philosopher, judge and teacher and is linked to the majestic oak. Although druids have long been associated with stone circles, their primary place of worship is the sacred grove. Druidry is a type of nature-worship, to employ a general description and like many pagan paths is currently growing in popularity.

Dryads

Dryads were tree-spirits, one of the varieties of the old Greek nature spirits, guardians and personifications of the life of the tree and, in woodland, we may still sense their presence. In recent years some

different views of dryads and similar entities have emerged. These can be regarded as locations where the force field of the earth – probably a force that is electromagnetic electrostatic or where levels of background radiation may be higher – interact with the 'psyche-field' of an individual, resulting in the perception of ghosts or similar. Such places seem linked to the proximity of water, as if the water acts as a sort of film on which impressions of intense feelings or highly charged events are recorded, ready to be replayed in the right circumstance. Water is present in varying degrees beneath and around trees. These interesting ideas in no way diminish the mystery of dryads and are discussed in greater detail by Tom Graves in *Needles and Stone* (Gothic Image, 1986) and in *Ghost and Ghoul* (Routledge and Kegan Paul, 1961) and *Ghost and Divining Rod* (Routledge and Kegan Paul, 1963) by Tom Lethbridge.

Divination

Humans have long looked to the natural world for glimpses of hidden knowledge, as if we sense that the simplest, most unselfconscious forms of life can provide a gateway to something we can longer see. Trees are used in many divinational practices with the best known being the dowsing rod, made from a forked hazel twig, which twitches to reveal the presence of underground water. Runes can be carved on wood and thrown to obtain the answer to a question. Yvonne Aburrow, in *The Enchanted Forest* (see Further Reading), lists apple, ash, hazel, poplar, orange, rowan and witch-hazel as favoured woods for this. An apple can be cut in half as a love divination; an even number of seeds meaning marriage, an uneven number remaining single, one cut seed suggesting a problematic relationship and two cut seeds widowhood. Similarly an orange can provide the answer to a question, an even number of seeds meaning no, an odd number yes. The specific sound created by knocking on a tree – another meaning of 'knock on wood' – was used in divination. Such simple things as the fall of a twig or the shape of a branch, in a crucial place or time, could also be a 'sign'. Birds, who inhabit trees, were also considered to bring messages, an idea still alive in the rhyme about magpies:

> *One for sorrow, two for joy,*
> *Three for a girl, four for a boy,*
> *Five for silver, six for gold,*
> *Seven for a secret never to be told.*

I have certainly found the first two meanings have been borne out in my life – this doesn't mean that every single magpie brings bad luck, but when I have been in a questioning mood and have seen a lone magpie, it has generally portended some difficulty or concern, usually of a minor nature.

Divination is largely a matter that takes place within the consciousness of the diviner and incense is a potent aid to changes in consciousness. Tree materials are naturally used extensively in incense. One divination incense given by Scott Cunningham in The *Complete Book of Incense, Oils and Brews* (Llewellyn, 1991) consists of two parts of sandalwood, one part orange peel, one part mace and one part cinnamon – a fragrant combination.

Mistletoe

Although mistletoe does not grow easily on the oak, it was considered to be most sacred if found on this tree, the King of the Forest. This is seen by the druids as a magical occurrence, for the white mistle-berries are representative of the semen of the God and symbolise a special moment of the entry of Divinity into the world of Time. The mistletoe is lopped with a golden sickle from the tree at Yule – the gold of the sickle representing the masculine principle and the lunar shape of the sickle meaning the Feminine. It is caught in a cloth and pieces are distributed to all participants as a symbol of fertility – not merely physical fertility but also the mental fertility of wisdom. We still kiss under the mistletoe for luck. Holly and mistletoe are used as decorations at Christmas – the prickly energy of the holly with its fiery berries can be seen as protecting the precious life of the baby sun-god. Holly and ivy were held to be masculine and feminine respectively, and this is honoured in the carol *The Holly and the Ivy*, actually a celebration of nature and sexuality.

The Maypole

Dancing around the maypole was a spring custom in England at the start of May. The phallic, sexual symbolism of the pole and the bawdy celebrations that surrounded it were unacceptable to the seventeenth-century Puritans, but the custom was reinstated when Charles II was restored to the monarchy.

The basis of the maypole is that it represents the 'axis mundi' around which all creation turns. It can also be seen as the World Tree, uniting Heaven, Earth and Underworld – however it is defined its symbolism is cosmic and it is a powerful creative sign at the time of year when the mating of the Goddess and God is being celebrated. The spiralling feet of the dancers represent the passage of life, into and out of the manifest world. The maypole may have originated from the sacred pine beneath which the dying god Attis, in one version of his myth, castrated himself. After his death the god turned into a pine tree. Attis was the consort/grandson of Cybele, Anatolian Great Mother Goddess, and is one of many personifications of the sacrificial vegetation god. A pine would be cut down in honour of Cybele and decorated with an effigy of Attis to form the focus of orgiastic and bloody rites. Osiris was also associated with the pine and in some parts of Egypt his effigy was placed in a hollowed pine tree. The cone of the pine suggests phallic potency and these were traditionally affixed to the end of wands.

Another favourite tree for use as a maypole was the ash. Yggdrasil, the World Tree of Norse myth, was an ash. Ash symbolises the energy of the sky-god, conducted towards the earth. Whatever tree is used the meanings, essentially of the union of male and female, remain the same.

Going a-maying

The custom of going 'a-maying' meant gathering hawthorn, believed to be unlucky if brought indoors before May Eve. This often meant staying out all night and making love beneath the trees in the heady air laden with the scent of hawthorn blossom, a smell reminiscent of female secretions. Such sexual unions were called 'greenwood marriages'. Hawthorn is very much a tree associated with marriage, its white blossom decking it out like a spring bride.

Bonfires and needfires

Fire, which can be kindled by rubbing two pieces of wood together, was believed to originate in the heart of the wood itself. This was celestial fire, drawn down from the moon and gathered within the tree. Fires were built to celebrate the four major Celtic festivals of Samhain (31 October), Imbolc (2 February), Beltane (30 April) and Lughnasadh/Lammas (31 July). These festivals were based on the yearly rhythms of a herding people. Later the Equinoxes and Solstices were added and, indeed, all eight festivals are appropriately marked by fire, a transformative element that holds much fascination. These ceremonial fires were often held to have magical or healing properties, some of which had basis in fact – for instance, to rid them of winter infections, cattle were driven between two fires at Beltane. People would jump the Bel-fire for all sorts of good luck, fertility, mating and health. Fire brings the power of the sun to earth.

Effigies burnt within the fire are representations of the vegetation spirit or tree spirit – they echo the theme of sacrificial god and there can be no doubt that human sacrifice was at times rendered in this way. Guy Fawkes, whose effigy is burnt on 5 November, may be remembered as a would-be king-slayer. However, his memory is strengthened by a much older tradition of sacrificial kings. Sacrifices would often be made at Hallowe'en/Samhain, which is close to 5 November (times of festivity were not necessarily bound strictly to the calendar and in any case often spanned several days). At this time of growing darkness propitiation would sometimes be made to forces in nature that might be malevolent. It must be remembered, however, that the concept of sacrifice arises from a sense of fear and alienation from the natural world, and this may well have been a relative latecomer, not practised by earlier, goddess-worshipping societies who felt an instinctual union with the natural world.

Needfires were kindled at times of need, such as plague, when cattle would be driven through the flames to protect them. There were various rituals and taboos surrounding these fires, such as they must be kindled, by twins or a virgin, or that all other fires must be extinguished. Thus the magical property of the fire was honoured and fostered.

Wassailing

This is a ceremony, of ancient origin, observed in the British apple-growing areas of Somerset, Herefordshire and Kent. Apples were the food of the Celtic gods, with many Underworld and magical associations. Unicorns were said to dwell under apple trees. Apples and apple blossom can also mean love and peace. The saying 'An apple a day keeps the doctor away' has some basis in fact, for a good apple contains just about the daily minimum requirement of vitamin C. Apples are fermented to form cider, and herein may lie one secret of the apple's importance, for it may be that fermented apples were used to induce trance states, rather than for the modern recreation of getting drunk! Wassailing is a ceremony to 'wake up' the apple trees by singing, dancing and knocking on the tree trunks. Libations of cider are poured on the roots and later cider is drunk in considerable quantity by the merry wassailers! Wassailing is usually carried out in January, traditionally on Twelfth Night.

Touch wood

How many times do we touch wood, for luck, after we have made some statement about our hopes, needs and beliefs? People who would not call themselves superstitious still pat the table top, saying 'touch wood' after they have made mention of a cherished plan. Touching wood feels like a grounding action. It is in fact an ancient custom, derived from Celtic tradition, when the habit of touching wood was much more than the perfunctory tap that we resort to. In times of need they approached a loved tree and communed with it, 'touching' the spirit of the tree and obtaining healing, comfort and even enlightenment. Such trees were believed to house the spirits of the ancestors within them, or the gods and goddesses themselves. Tress were planted on burial mounds in order that the spirits of the deceased would live on within them and their wisdom be still accessible to the tribe.

The Tree of Life

The term 'Tree of Life' is used often quite loosely to refer to the symbology of the tree as representing all levels of existence, fertility, fruitfulness, cyclicity, the meandering branches representing the variations of life and its choices and possibilities. However, the Tree of Life is, strictly speaking, a notion from The Jewish mystical doctrine of the Qabalah. It is also called the Ets Chayyim. Best

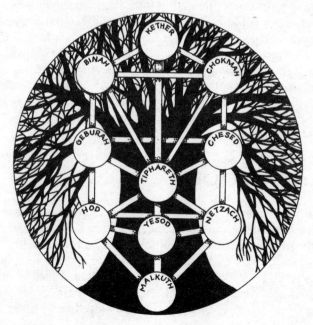

understood as a diagram of manifestation, it is a blueprint of the process of any activity or situation. It can be seen as the make-up of an individual, or a map of the universe, starting with purest energy and descending to physical form.

The Tree of Life is made up of ten Sephiroth (singular Sephira) or spheres and the twenty-two paths that connect and interconnect between them. Each of the spheres is equated with a planet. Kether = Neptune, Tiphareth = Sun, Yesod = Moon, Malkuth = Earth, Binah = Saturn, Geburah = Mars, Hod = Mercury, Chokmah = Uranus, Chesed = Jupiter and Netzach = Venus. Daath, the Hidden One, below Kether and above Tiphareth is said to correspond to Pluto.

The properties of each Sephira are linked with the astrological meanings of the planets and with an extensive system of correspondences used in rituals on the 'like attracts like' basis. These can embrace many factors – plants, colours, directions, numbers, creatures, concepts – which are felt to harmonise. For instance, a spell for fertility might incorporate The Moon, herbs such as willow and lemon balm, Monday, the goddess Bride and the High Priestess tarot card. However, there is more at work here than a simplistic belief that burning certain herbs on a certain day by the light of the full moon will bring about a specific result (although it is surprising how effective this can be!). Correspondences are also a memory aid, activating a train of associations in the mind of the practitioner and connecting her or him to the cosmic web. They are a thing of beauty, bringing the universe to life and stimulating the mind. The Celtic system of Ogham is also a system of correspondences – an alphabet linked to many trees, not just one. The tree is also symbolic of the many nerve branches and endings that are fired off within the skull – interestingly, the 'branches' or dendrites between brain cells grow physically when we think.

The twenty-two paths of the Tree of Life are each associated with a card in the Major Arcana of the tarot pack. The Tree of Life is also a diagram of the human psyche and so these paths can be travelled by 'pathworking' – a system of guided visualisation or trancework. There is an important saying 'All the Sephiroth are equally holy'. Kether, the crown of the tree is equal, not superior, to Malkuth at the foot. Root is just as important as topmost branch, spirituality is no more valuable and meaningful than physical form, for they are interdependent, part of a totality, part of the great Tree.

The sacred tree

There are many myths about trees with special gifts and properties. Irish legend tells of Connla's magic well, around which grew the nine hazels of wisdom and poetry. These dropped nuts into the water to be eaten by the sacred salmon – those who desired the gift of knowledge sought to eat the nuts or the salmon. Greek myth tells of the Garden of the Hesperides, where there grew a sacred apple tree whose fruit bestowed immortality. Nine maidens, the Hesperides, protected this tree while a serpent coiled about its roots – these apples belonged to the goddess of love. The serpent has long been symbolic of wisdom and its spiralling movements signify the passage into and out of the manifest world and back into manifestation once more. With its cyclical sloughing off of its skin, the serpent is linked to female sexual cycles and their attendant gifts of enlightenment that arise from the different states of consciousness available to women. The nine Hesperides are one of several groupings of three or three-times-three goddesses, arising from the Triple Goddess, Maiden, Mother and Crone. The sacred tree is the 'omphalos', or world centre. In truth the omphalos is wherever we are at a given time, signifying the reality of our incarnation and our bearings in the material world.

The biblical story tells of the Tree of Life and the Tree of Knowledge that grow in Paradise. The Tree of Life is at the centre and it signifies cyclicity, rebirth and a state of primal innocence that blends with the perfection of the natural world. It is a symbol of unity whereas the Tree of Knowledge represents duality – 'good and evil'. Adam and Eve reside in Paradise but after Eve tempts Adam with the forbidden apple God drives them out of the Garden as a punishment. The serpent is depicted as an evil force that seduces Eve as she in turn seduces Adam. This is a subversion of earlier myths, which portray the serpent as a guardian of wisdom and Woman as the priestess, the initiate of the Mysteries. We could interpret the tale of the Garden

of Eden as a patriarchal take-over of the territories of the ancient mother goddess. However, there are also other meanings, for the two trees can signify different states of consciousness through which humans must pass to reach enlightenment. The Tree of Life, of the blissful state of primal oneness, can be taken to mean the human condition in a primitive Dreamtime, when there is a blending with Nature, but little detached consciousness. The Tree of Knowledge confers a consciousness of being separate, having an ego, a power to reflect and thus an ability to experience alienation, fear and suffering. Eating from this Tree is, perhaps, a necessary passage on the way to a more fully integrated consciousness that embraces also a sense of unique identity and also a sense of union with the cosmic web. This is a dangerous transition and one that the human race still struggles with, looking for scapegoats and groping our way back towards the Garden. However, the image of the Sacred Tree is always before us, showing us the way and, if a new consciousness is to dawn for us, it will rise like the sun from its ancient branches.

Trees and shamanism

Shamanism is the oldest spiritual discipline known to humans. Put simply it is the art of 'spirit flight' where the shaman enters a trance state and leaves the physical body for the subtle realms, there to glean valuable information and insight. In earlier times the purpose of spirit flight would usually have been to gather knowledge helpful to the tribe – unlike the trance state of mediumship, where the practitioner is taken over by other entities, the shamanic out-of-body journey always has a purpose. In shamanism it is the shaman her- or himself who is in control. Shamanic practices are being adapted for modern people and increasingly explored in groups and lodges by those seeking direct experience of the transcendent. (See *Shamanism – A Beginner's Guide* in this series).

Basic to the practice of shamanism is a deep regard for nature and a belief that all is alive and worthy of respect – crystals, rocks, trees and animals all have a type of life unique to themselves and vibrate at their own rate. The earth herself is alive. The shaman sees herself as part of the cosmic tapestry. In shamanism the help of totem or power animals is sought, for these are potent, living symbols of abilities we may wish to emulate. Trees, too, may be active as totems providing a pathway into the heart and mystery of nature and the spirit. It is possible that the venerable shamanic tradition of the Druids incorporated trees as totems and gateways to the hidden realms, the soul of the tree giving guidance and inspiration to the Druid on shamanic flight.

Shamanic traditions include concepts of cosmology – a type of map of the ethereal realms – and it is here that the presence of the tree becomes especially important as many cosmologies were based on the World Tree. Shamanic journeys traverse Middleworld, Upperworld and Lowerworld. The first is closest to the day-to-day world, but unfettered by restraints of space and time, the second is the realm of widest perspective, inhabited by celestial goddesses and gods and the third is the home of ancestral spirits, often the 'power house' of subconscious elements, inhabited by underworld entities

that we may fear, where we can obtain our greatest source of potency. The World Tree spans these three realms; branches in Upperworld, trunk in Middleworld and roots snaking down into Lowerworld. Shamanic journeys are usually triggered by drumbeat and the drum is often called the 'shaman's horse'. Traditionally, this drum was seen as being made from the wood of the World Tree itself and often showed drawings of the Tree. Sometimes the tribal shaman would ascend an actual tree as a metaphor for his inner journey up into the branches of the World Tree. Indeed, one of the meanings behind stories of witches riding broomsticks is that of 'riding' a branch of the World Tree while in spirit flight, and many traditional tales, such as that of Jack and the Beanstalk, are cryptic accounts of shamanic journeys.

In *Shamanism; Archaic Techniques of Ecstasy* (Arkana, 1989) Mircea Eliade tells us that the Siberian Yakut '... believe that at the "golden navel of the earth" stands a tree with eight branches; it rises in a sort of primordial paradise, for there the first man was born and he feeds on the milk of a woman who half emerges from the trunk of the tree'. Other tribes believed that the souls of little children perch like birds on the branches of the Cosmic Tree, waiting to be born. Other motifs include the idea of a Tree with a million leaves on each of which a human fate is inscribed. Eliade explains:

> *Several religious ideas are implied in the symbolism of the World Tree ... it represents the universe in continual regeneration, the inexhaustible spring of cosmic life ... it symbolises the sky or the planetary heavens ... in a number of archaic traditions the Cosmic Tree, expressing the sacrality of the world ... is related ... to the idea of absolute reality and immortality ... Enriched by innumerable mythical doublets and complementary symbols (Woman, the Wellspring, Milk, Animals, Fruits etc.) the Cosmic Tree always presents itself as the very reservoir of life and the master of destinies.*

One of the best known World Trees is the Scandinavian Yggdrasil. Growing from Hel, the Lowerworld, through Midgard and rising into the Upperworld, the realms of Asgard and the dwelling place of the Aesir, or Norse gods. The god Odin ties horse to this Tree, in common with gods who do similarly in other pantheons – reinforcing connection between the Tree and the travelling ability of the steed.

In an initiatory experience, Odin hung upon Yggdrasil until he received the secret of the runes in a shamanic revelation. Such hanging was symbolically incorporated into many archaic rites of initiation. The idea of 'hanging' suspended between the worlds is a notable metaphor for the surrendering of one's power to act, hanging like a leaf upon the tree, awaiting the winds of fate, sacrificing oneself, as the vegetable world regularly does and by so doing to obtain incomparable insight. These are themes are echoed in the meaning of the The Hanged Man tarot card. There also links with the sacrificial vegetation god and even Christ's crucifixion. In all cases the Tree offers a passage to a deeper understanding, to experiences of an other-worldly nature that are nonetheless relevant to this world, wherein the mighty trunk of the Tree appears. Thus the symbol of the Tree unifies spirit and matter and offers a pathway between the worlds. We are able, in a subtle way perhaps, to perceive trees in such a manner – hence part of their enchantment.

Some tree festival days

Tu B'shvat – the Jewish New Year of the trees, celebrated at the full moon of January/February. Qabalists see this as the time that the Tree of Life renews the flow of vitality into the manifest world, celebrated in a variety of ways, with fruits and tree-planting.

Arbor Day – observed in Britain on 29 May.

Apple Day – celebrated on 21 October or on the nearest weekend, Apple Day celebrates the variety of fruits provided and focuses on the preservation of old orchards. It is usually a spontaneous festival, created by people in their own locality – places where this is celebrated include Holland, France, Tasmania, USA and Britain.

Tree Dressing Day – this demonstrates that trees are valued and cared for and is inspired by the old customs of dressing trees. It takes place on the first weekend in December.

National Tree Week – observed for ten days in Britain, culminating in the first Sunday in December. A time for nationwide tree events of all descriptions.

PRACTICE – CREATING A TREE CEREMONY

In this chapter we have explored many traditional meanings of trees and looked at some of the well-known customs associated with them. We are rediscovering our relationship with trees and learning to value them. It is appropriate that we may wish to construct fresh rituals, in keeping with our lives today, to affirm our connection with the world of trees.

Your tree ceremony can incorporate song, dance, drama, symbolic action, poetry and feasting. One very simple action is for a group of people participating to hold hands and dance, or circle, around the tree. The ceremony may be about seasonal observance, celebrational, healing, or may centre on the planting of a tree, covering many themes. Make sure that the ceremony you devise has a beginning, a middle and an end, and, if there are a number of people taking part, encourage each person to develop their own contribution.

As you make your plans, meditate and envelop yourself in the purpose of your ceremony. What comes to mind? Jot down anything at all that occurs to you, for you can refine it later. Don't reason yourself out of any ideas. Research the lore, mythology and traditional qualities associated with the tree. Make sure you are also well-informed about practical matters – for instance, if planting a tree have you chosen the right position and season? You will need a follow-on plan to tend the tree, if it is to survive. Even if all other conditions are correct, there is little point planting a tree where it will be vandalised or eaten by animals.

A good start to many rituals could be to hold hands around the tree, or planting site, and to state your intention in the coming ceremony. Then proceed with the 'meaty' bit, which could include many of the elements mentioned, such as dramatic enactments of myth or simple actions, song and dance. Finish as you started, holding hands and slowly circling the tree, while concentrating on your purpose and communing with the tree. As a simple example, you might want to hang an object on a tree as an offering, a gesture of letting go or to ease passage into a new state of being. Choose something biodegradable – for instance you might place a harvest cake in the branches, to the delight of the birds, or tie a cotton ribbon around a branch, for a wish. I'm sure I do not need to remind you not to cause litter or damage! Anything connected with a tree is likely to mean growth, or transmutation. If you wish to leave something well and truly behind you, best to write it on a shed leaf and cast it into running water.

It is good to involve children in the venture, small children will, quite happily, enter into almost anything. Use story, song and playful participation. Each child may like to bring a handful of earth from their own garden. Young children have a short attention span – a variety of short activities will keep them interested longer than something extensive. After about the age of seven, many children become logical and sceptical – do not invite scorn by asking them to go along with what they may find absurd! For instance, a local custom was revived at a school near me by a headteacher conscious of the value of old ceremonies. However, rapping on trees and chanting 'Bud well, bear well, wake up in the morning' went down like a lead balloon with sophisticated ten year olds! Encourage scientific interest in the properties of the trees. Some children may enjoy taking part in dramas such as a re-enactment of Holly King/Oak King and some children may play music or compose poetry. Involve older children in planning the ceremony. If you wish to make forays into the esoteric, keep well grounded, perhaps referring to J.E. Lovelock's concept of Gaia. If you are fortunate enough to be able to interest teenagers in your plans, let them bring their own vitality, zest and music – that's what it's all about!

TREES AND MAGIC

On Midsummer's Eve
We hasten to weave
Fern and leaf
For every grief,
Stalk and seed
For every need

Valerie Worth, *Herb-Gathering Charm*

Magic is a transformative act and true transformation occurs deep in our roots. Real inner change is not at all easy to achieve, for somehow we tend to revert to type – although we think of ourselves as 'free' we are actually prisoners of our conditioning and unconscious responses. Any genuine shift in consciousness will change our environment and experiences, working real magic. In many ways trees have the power to help us change our consciousness – their presence invites it, the aroma of a living tree, or incense, stimulates it and their many time-honoured associations show the paths to magic.

Magic has been defined as 'the art of changing consciousness at will' or 'the art of causing change to occur in conformity with the will' – these definitions come from the magician, Aleister Crowley. Magic is often doubted by those who possess a linear consciousness and believe there is only one way to go about things, that all connections are direct cause and effect. To the practitioner of magic, however, desire and focus are given more weight than direct action with magical changes occurring first on the inner planes, the invisible essence that underlies creation. The idea that a small action, such as waving a wand or chanting a spell, could have a dramatic effect mirrors modern theories, such as the Chaos theory, where the flutter of a butterfly's wings on one side of the earth can affect the weather on the other side. All actions have a knock-on effect and when they are backed by specific intention their force is compounded. Rupert Sheldrake's idea of morphogenetic fields also suggests that life does not exist simply in the visible, material world, but is underpinned by unseen 'fields' that carry the blue-print, or essence, of a life-form. It is at such an essential level that magic operates. Trees, as a connection to the primeval power of the natural world, have magical properties of which we can avail ourselves.

Trees and witches

The lore of the witch springs from soil and stone, moon-glow, cloud-drift and the seasonal rhythm, so it is no wonder that the associations between witches and trees are fundamental. To the witch there is great power in nature and especially in trees. Witches were reputed to be able to disguise themselves as trees, the elder and the thorn tree are two trees noted for this. A well-known story, in this respect, concerns the Rollright Stones in Oxfordshire which are said originally to have been a Danish king and his knights on their way to fight for the crown of England. This king had the ill-wisdom to ask a witch what his fate might be and was turned to stone by the words:

> *...Rise up stick and stand still stone,*
> *For King of England thou shalt be none,*
> *Thou and thy men hoar stones shall be,*
> *And I myself an elder tree*

Elder has associations with the Germanic underworld Goddess, Hela, and it has close links with feminine power, for when cut it bleeds red sap, like menstrual blood. Although the idea may be unpopular in a male-dominated society, the menstrual time is a sacred time, when a woman may commune with her hidden self and, while no human child is to be, yet now is the birth of the magical child, when a woman may be more open to shamanic experience and inner renewal. All such experience is the realm of the witch and wise-woman and may be made use of, magically. Flutes made from elder were said to be able to summon spirits and elder-blossom can be worn for a similar purpose. If you wish to see the hosts of Faerie, stand under an elder tree on Midsummer's Night and breathe deep the heady incense vapour of the flowers – but make sure you are carrying something made of iron or you may disappear forever! The elder tree can be kissed by pregnant women for good fortune for the baby and elder berries placed underneath the pillow are said to promote peaceful sleep. The elder has powers to reverse evil magic and was also thought to have been the wood from which Christ's cross was fashioned, as well as the tree from which Judas hanged himself. Elder has a dual aspect, for it can also be used to detect witches – by dabbing the green juice on the eyelids of a Christian all witches were revealed, which was a handy belief in times of persecution when a witch-finder often benefited financially from the denunciation of an unfortunate (but well-off) suspect.

The Elder Mother has potent energy, with which she protects the country nooks which are her domain and there are traditional warnings about the use of elder. Permission should always be asked of the elder tree – as with any tree – before cutting the wood or the spirit of the tree may follow you. Jacqueline Memory Paterson (see Further Reading) quotes this old rhyme to placate Elder Mother:

> *Owd Girl, give me of thy wood.*
> *An' I will give thee some of mine.*
> *When I become a tree*

Some sources state that pre-reformation churches were often built on ancient sacred pagan sites and an elder tree found growing in a churchyard is magically potent. To charm warts, cut a small green twig from it while the moon is waning, rub the warts with the twig and bury it where it may rot away, so taking the warts with it – and if my own record at wart-charming is anything to go by you may need to do this several times!

Hawthorn is part of the 'fairy triad' of oak, ash and thorn. Witches were said to dance and perform their rites close to the branches of the thorn tree and where the fairy triad is found there one may catch a glimpse of the people of Faerie. This particular combination of trees was used by the Druids in certain rites. From the oak comes the strength and firmness of the Masculine, from the thorn emanates the intuition and creativity of the Feminine and the ash combines and directs these two. Hawthorn, sacred to the White Goddess, should traditionally only be brought indoors on May Eve. Blackthorn, which flowers earlier, is sacred to the Dark Goddess and lore states that this should not be brought indoors at all, for fear of Her anger. However, to take such an attitude to this goddess-aspect is really to subscribe to patriarchal prejudice which regards certain aspects of the Feminine as highly suspect. The Dark Goddess is no malevolent destructress but simply She who brings endings, in wisdom and kindly season, in order that new life may proceed.

Blackthorn staffs were used for cursing and both blackthorn and hawthorn afford psychic protection when grown as hedges or thickets. Hawthorn is said to cheer depression when carried. Like elder, hawthorn connects with the realm of Otherworld and to sit beneath a hawthorn at Beltane, Midsummer or Samhain is to invite abduction by faeries. A well-known hawthorn spell goes like this:

> *The fair maid who the first of May,*
> *Goes to the fields at break of day*
> *And walks in dew from the hawthorn tree*
> *Will ever handsome be.*

The sacred grove

While there are many specific associations in folk-lore between elder, thorn and witches, all trees are potential conductors of the magical. Magical rites are held within a magic circle – a 'world between the worlds' that offers both protection and containment and is constructed upon the subtle plane by a combination of ritual and visualisation. To strengthen the circle, guardians or elemental powers are called upon at the four quarters of the circle; North, South, East and West. While traditions vary, the usual associations are South with Fire, West with Water, North with Earth and East with Air – readers in the Southern Hemisphere may prefer to reverse the North/South associations, as for you the sun remains in the north. For rites it is usual to have a representation of all the elements upon the altar and/or within the circle. As their boughs sigh and whisper in the breeze, trees may be taken as potent representatives of the Air element reaching up towards the heavens. Any rituals designed to evoke freedom, clear thought and inspiration can be most appropriately performed within a grove of trees.

However, as magical rites are generally best performed out of doors (practical considerations always born in mind!) a grove of trees lends itself especially well to this sort of activity. The auras of the trees themselves are protective and inspiring and conducive to shifts in the state of consciousness. If the site is well chosen the trees may offer a natural circle, or clear space. Beech trees, with their long trunks and high branches often provide an especially favourable location. Practitioners working outside may like to mark their circle with birdseed, as suggested by Philip Heselton in *Secret Places of the Goddess* (see Further Reading) – or you may chose a 'fairy ring'. Full instructions for the formation of the magic circle are outside the scope of this book, but you may like to consult *Witchcraft – A Beginner's Guide* in this series, for further information.

The eight pagan festivals are celebrated in a variety of ways by modern pagans and while some traditions preclude the working of magic at the Festivals – as these are times of reverence and festivity – others do include magical workings where appropriate. I feel that, for a busy person, to have set aside the time for a ritual and taken trouble with preparation, it is a good idea to accomplish as much as feels comfortable. In any case, a true celebration of the festivals is, in itself, an act of magic. The passage of the seasons is graphically portrayed by trees in all their moods and appearances and so they provide a beautiful and evocative ritual setting.

The idea of the 'sacred grove' is principally associated with Druids, the 'wise men of the trees', who use the power of trees to connect with the spirit of nature and thus their own profound essence. All trees and plants are held sacred by the Druids, and so the 'grove' can be composed of a selection of many diverse trees. The twenty-five trees of the Ogham alphabet, discussed later, were held in especial veneration. The three grades of the Druid tradition – Bards, Ovates and Druids – are specifically associated with the birch, the yew and the oak, respectively. Another important selection of trees may be the thirteen associated with the Celtic tree calendar, also discussed later. The selection of the thirteen does vary somewhat from source to source, and I am sure that more than one tree may be associated with a certain time of the year.

The sacred grove may have many components and many meanings and it is possible that certain groves have been tended over many hundreds of years in traditions, whose true significance may have become obscured. Whatever the case, the tree grove is a true pagan cathedral, a dwelling-place of the awesome and ancient earth spirit. It is up to each individual to make contact with this in the way, and with the trees, that she or he finds most 'special'.

ThE MAGIC WANd

Portrayed in children's books waved by Fairy Godmothers and magicians, the wand is usually seen with stars and sparks twinkling at the tip. Like many snippets from fable, the wand is actually factual and forms an inherent part of most magical traditions. The wand aids concentration and focus and its tip, waving in the air, has a mesmerising effect. The wand is associated by some with the Fire

element as it seems to be connected with transformation and inspiration, although there are others who equate it with air. Really it is a matter of what feels right to the practitioner.

There are several traditional ways to go about obtaining your wand. Some state that a wand should never be cut but only taken from fallen wood. Another way is to walk until you find a tree that 'feels' right and then ask it if you may take a branch. Another – and perhaps the best – way is to get to know your tree over a period of time by sitting close to it and partaking its essence. Then in time you will develop a bond with the tree and will know when it is right to cut your wand. Afterwards, every time you look at or touch your wand, all the potency and wisdom of the tree will instantly fill your consciousness.

Depending upon what uses you intend, wands can be made of almost any tree. Celtic wands were made of hazel, a mercurial tree for quick results and blinding intuitive flashes. The Gaelic white wand was of yew, slow growing, ancient and wise as the Nature Goddess Herself. Wands for moon magic can be of willow, and I have a simple little willow wand that I found which serves to connect me with the flowing enchantment of the full moon. Druid's wands were made of ash and used for healing. Ash is connected both to the male and female principles, to sun and water and to communication over the waves. Merlin's wand was reputed to be of oak – a commanding and steadfast tree. Rowan wands are protective. Wands can be tipped with an acorn or pine cones, so that they are phallic in appearance. The traditional associations of a tree – as covered later in 'Selection of Trees' – can be a guide as to usage. Far better is to take the trouble to get to know the tree and its dryad spirit, so that your wand is both part of you and a living connection to the wisdom of the trees.

Broomsticks

The connection between witches and broomsticks is real and not confined to bedtime stories and medieval superstition. Witches use a besom ritually, to cleanse an area before creating a magic circle. 'Riding on a broomstick' is a metaphor for shamanic, ecstatic journeys, where the witch is, in a sense, riding on the branches of the World Tree. The broom, with its phallic handle plunged deep into feminine brush, unites the female and the male, symbolically and of course riding a broomstick also represents sexual ecstasy, which is closely allied to states of trance. It may well be that witches smeared the broom with 'flying ointment' – a combination of trance-inducing herbs – and used the broom-handle to administer the ointment to the delicate genital tissues. To the witch sex is sacred and sexual energy is magically potent, a divine gift, to be appreciated, enjoyed and respected.

The broomstick can be made from several woods and, like the wand, will accordingly lend itself better to certain tasks. Birch twigs used in the broom are said to be most 'aerodynamic' as the branches of the birch are always a-stir on the tree. A handle of hazel is visionary and apple aids workings to do with love and fertility. The original household broom was of the actual broom plant, *Planta genista*, the badge of the Plantagenet family who were rumoured to favour the Old Religion of witchcraft and nature-worship. Brooms were 'ridden' over the fields to ensure a prolific crop and couples jumped the broomstick at weddings and handfastings. Today, witches still use broomsticks for ritual purposes and the staff of the broom may be adorned with woven cords or symbols as the user prefers.

Incense

The burning of incense alters the atmosphere profoundly and immediately and is the backdrop to most rituals. The aroma speaks directly to the primitive corners of the psyche and connects us to the plant essences that are evaporating in a way that is unutterably ancient. Choice of plants for incense depends to some extent on the relevant associations and your own preferences. Incense is covered fully in *Herbs for Magic and Ritual – A Beginner's Guide* in this series. Below are examples of a few incense blends.

- **Fire of Azrael incense**   This is one of the most famous blends, given by Dion Fortune in *The Sea Priestess* (Aquarian, 1989), made of juniper, sandalwood and cedar. This incense gives revelation and insight into past lifetimes. Combine 25 g (1 oz) crushed juniper berries, 25 g (1 oz) small chips of sandalwood and a similar proportion of cedarwood chips or, if not available, use ten drops of cedarwood essential oil.
- **Purification**   Pine, juniper and cedar.
- **General**   Frankincense, cinnamon, myrrh.
- **To honour the Mother Goddess**   Rose, frankincense, cypress.
- **Meditation**   Gum Acacia (or Arabic), sandalwood.
- **Love**   Rose, sandalwood, apple blossom, willow, broom, lavender.
- **Prosperity**   Frankincense, cinnamon, lemon (or lemon balm), orange peel, mace, copal.
- **Protection**   Frankincense, myrrh, clove.

As with all magical activities it is important to experiment, to make contact with your instincts and to go with what you feel works for you.

Spells

There are many specific spells associated with trees. Below are a few simple spells to try.

- **Protection while travelling**   Place a leaf from an ash tree in the car or on the seat of a motorcycle.
- **Love**   Cut an apple in two crosswise so you can see the five-point star at the centre which is special to the Mother Goddess. Eat half and give your lover the other half, for a connection that will never be severed.
- **Healing**   Most trees will give healing to body and spirit simply by their presence. Jacqueline Memory Paterson suggests specifically chewing a few hawthorn leaves slowly and imagining the healing power of this tree being absorbed. However, **always be sure you know it is hawthorn, for some trees are poisonous**.
- **To banish negativity**   Add pine needles or essential oil to bath water and imagine all grumpiness and misery going down the drain.

- **To make a wish come true**   Carve the words of the wish on a beech twig. Write the wish on a bay leaf and burn it.
- **For creativity**   Carry beech wood or leaves.
- **To increase psychic powers**   Carry rowan wood.
- **To attract money**   Carry poplar leaves or buds. Plant an acorn at the dark of the moon. As the moon waxes so your money will grow.
- **Fertility**   To increase fertility carry a pine cone.
- **To keep a job**   Shell and eat pecan nuts while picturing yourself remaining at the job and loving it! Then put the shells in a bag and keep them somewhere safe.
- **For the answer to a question**   Think about the question while eating an orange. Then count the seeds. An even number mean no, an odd number yes.
- **For health and longevity**   Carry an acorn.
- **For potency**   Carry an acorn.
- **To protect against sorcery**   Carry larch.
- **To attract the opposite sex**   Carry cloves – this also comforts the bereaved.
- **For prophetic dreams**   Place bay leaves under the pillow.

3

A YEAR OF TREES

Crashing among the boughs
folk heard Woden himself
giddy with rune-making

Paul Matthews, *The Ground That Love Sees*

WE have seen in earlier chapters how Odin/Woden received the wisdom of the runes while hanging on the World Tree, Yggdrasil. As well as being symbols for use in magic and divination Runes are an alphabet – indeed, there is a magical aspect to the basic concept of an alphabet, for being able to write things down has a profound effect on human consciousness. Until relatively recently writing has been restricted to an elite – mostly the priestly caste – in recognition of its power. Each rune corresponds with a specific tree as in some cases the association of trees with alphabets is most ancient. Trees are the guardians of our race memory and collective consciousness and they complement us, on a vibrational level – a fact appreciated instinctively by our forebears.

Even more closely related to trees is the Celtic Ogham alphabet which was discovered, according to legend, by Ogmios, god of writing. This script encoded the wealth of tree-knowledge possessed by the Druids, and mystery and controversy still attend it. Ogham was inscribed on wood and stone and is quite possibly of pre-Celtic origin. Each stroke of the Ogham script corresponds to a letter in the alphabet and represents the first letter of the corresponding tree. Different sources give somewhat different associations. The alphabetical listing on page 37 follows that given by Philip Carr-Gomm in *The Druid Tradition* (see Further Reading) and includes the twenty-five trees and plants held as especially sacred by the Druids.

According to the poet and scholar Robert Graves, in his book *The White Goddess* (Faber and Faber, 1988), the thirteen major consonants of this alphabet were connected with the thirteen lunar months of the year and formed a calendar of seasonal tree-magic. Graves' theory has been contested by many critics who say there is no hard evidence to back his claims. However, with what we do know of the cosmological associations of trees and their many correspondences, seasonal and otherwise, it does seem reasonable that such links would have been made and have formed the basis for much other interpretation. As Philip Carr-Gomm puts it:

> *There has been much controversy as to whether the Ogham really was used as a calendar by the Druids, linking each tree and letter of the alphabet to a moon month, as suggested by Robert Graves. Whilst it is important to be aware that there is controversy, it is also important to understand that Druidry is evolving, and if they didn't correlate them in 500BC they do now – if it was Robert Graves' invention, then he was acting as a Druid when he did so – he was inspired, in other words. Someone has to invent things, or 'receive' them from the invisible world, and just because he or she does so in AD 1948 rather than BC 1948 is … unimportant to those of us who want to use Druidry as a living system …*

This 'living system' is also important to those seeking new dimensions of astrological understanding, for if each part of the year

The Ogham Alphabet

Letter	Irish name	Tree
B	beith	birch
L	luis	rowan
F	fearn	alder
S	saille	willow
N	nuinn	ash
H	huathe	hawthorn
D	duir	oak
T	tinne	holly
C	coll	hazel
Q	quert	apple
M	muinn	vine
G	gort	ivy
NG	ngetal	broom/fern (reed)
STR	straif	blackthorn
R	ruis	elder
A	ailm	fir/pine
O	onn	gorse
U	ur	heather
E	edhadh	aspen
I	ido	yew
EA	ebhadh	aspen
OI	oir	spindle
UI	uileand	honeysuckle
IO	iphin	gooseberry
AE	phagos	beech

Seasonal calendar of 13 trees ≈ the 13 lunar months

tree goddesses ~ Embla (Elder)

O-ryu (willow) Zemyna (oak)

Asheran (ash) Duan (hazel)

Kupalo (birch) Fauni (rowan)

Midwinter solstice ~ yew ~ dec 21

ruis ... beth ...

ngetal ... elder ... birch ... luis

reed ... nov 28 - oct 27 nov 24 - nov 25 - dec 22 dec 24 - jan 20 jan 21 - feb 17 feb 18 - mar 17 rowan ... nuin

gort ... reed ... sept 23 rowan ... ash ...

vine ... ash ... alder ... mar 18 - apr 14

muin ... autumn equinox ~ aspen ~ sept 2 - sept 29 hazel ... willow ... alder ... spring equinox ~ gorse ~ mar 21

coll ... hawthorn oak ... saille ... apr 15 - may 12

tinne ... duir ... holly nion ... may 13 - jun 9 jun 10 - jul 7

summer solstice ~ jun 21 ~ heather jul 8 - aug 4 aug 5 - sept 1

celtic tree calendar

© Mick Moon Designs 1994 & dedicated to the Goddess

4 festival trees represent the sun's position throughout the year

correlates with a tree, and the characteristics of that tree, what does it mean for a person born at that time? In the following section we shall be looking at each of the thirteen 'birth trees' and what they mean.

Thirteen Birth Trees

In this, several considerations need to be borne in mind. Firstly, when we divide the year up according to the movements of the moon we run into the problem that has bedevilled calendar-makers from time immemorial – lunar and solar cycles do not coincide. Further, there is more than one lunar cycle. The moon's thirteen rounds of the zodiac do not correspond exactly to the sun's single round, for the moon's thirteen circuits take about 364 days, leaving one intercalary day in a non-leap year. In addition, the lunar cycle from new to full and back to new again is distinct from the zodiac cycle, being a manifestation of the interrelationship between sun, moon and earth. This cycle takes twenty-nine and a half days, so most years have thirteen new or full moons, but never both. Sun and moon correspond exactly only every nineteen years, when there is a new moon at the Winter Solstice – called a Great Lunar Year in ancient belief, when the forces of the universe were renewed by the sacred cosmic marriage of sun and moon. December 1992 saw the start of the most recent Great Year for the Northern Hemisphere, for the Southern Hemisphere this could be regarded as starting six months earlier at the June Solstice, which is the Winter Solstice for the South. For our interpretation, the point here is that while we may interpret our birth-tree-month using thirteen divisions of the solar cycle, this probably bears no relationship to the position and phase of the moon when we were born. Indeed, I feel it is probable that the Druidic tree and lunar calendar really was at one time lunar, related to new and full moons rather than the solar cycle. This is not the practice today but the thirteen-fold division is at least a salute to the cycles of the moon.

For those of you living in the Southern Hemisphere a further consideration needs to be borne in mind – this calendar is seasonal, and while one might argue for associating a tree with several different parts of the year, or using different trees (and a variety of trees have been apportioned to the same time of the year by different authors), the basis of the tree calendar is Northern Hemisphere and, most properly for the Southern Hemisphere, needs to be moved on or back six months. Thus I have given alternative dates for Southern Hemisphere readers.

Finally, a tree calendar differs, in my opinion, from the traditional zodiac in that it emphasises avenues for growth, meditation and expansion of the imagination. Use your Tree not only to describe yourself, but to inspire you. Follow its symbolism, seek it out in woodland and see what further ideas come to you as a result.

The tree calendar – Northern Hemisphere

- **Birch** 24 Dec–20 Jan
- **Rowan** 21 Jan–17 Feb
- **Ash** 18 Feb–17 Mar
- **Alder** 18 Mar–14 Apr
- **Willow** 15 Apr–12 May
- **Hawthorn** 13 May–9 Jun
- **Oak** 10 Jun–7 Jul

- **Holly** 8 Jul–4 Aug
- **Hazel** 5 Aug–1 Sep
- **Vine** 2 Sep–29 Sep
- **Ivy** 30 Sep–27 Oct
- **Reed** 28 Oct–24 Nov
- **Elder** 25 Nov–23 Dec

The tree calendar – Southern Hemisphere

For those of you living in the Southern Hemisphere, I would suggest the following dates. If you live in a tropical, or sub-tropical, location where these trees are not native, they can still be of significance to you if you are of European, Anglo-Saxon or Celtic ancestry.

- **Birch** 24 Jun–21 Jul
- **Rowan** 22 Jul–18 Aug
- **Ash** 19 Aug–15 Sep
- **Alder** 16 Sep–13 Oct
- **Willow** 14 Oct–10 Nov
- **Hawthorn** 11 Nov–8 Dec
- **Oak** 9 Dec–5 Jan

- **Holly** 6 Jan–2 Feb
- **Hazel** 3 Feb–2 Mar
- **Vine** 3 Mar–30 Mar
- **Ivy** 31 Mar–27 Apr
- **Reed** 28 Apr–25 May
- **Elder** 26 May–23 Jun

BEITH – BIRCH MOON

Latin name *Betula pendula/alba*   **Family** *Betulaceae*
Other names Silver Birch, Lady of the Woods
Rune Berkana ᛒ
Celtic symbol The White Stag
Deities Venus, Frigga
Other associations Mysteries of the Maiden
goddess, earth, air and water elements. Healing and fresh starts.

Besides being an exceptionally graceful tree, the birch is extremely hardy. Its affinity with water encourages the growth of flowers and fungi beneath it, notably the fly agaric mushroom, which was used in Siberia to promote states of shamanic trance – perhaps it is because of this that the birch is considered the cosmic tree in some traditions. The birch can live for over ninety years and grows to 24 metres (80 feet) in height. The leaves appear at the start of spring and are an 'ace of spades' shape. Both female and male flowers appear on the same tree.

Birchwood is heavy and was used for casks, clogs, arrow-shafts and many other uses. Its wood is used to produce plywood and its bark has been used as parchment since ancient times. Native Americans use the bark to make canoes. Birch water is collected, while the sap is rising, by boring a small hole in the trunk into which a straw is inserted – this is only done for two days to avoid harming the tree. This can be used to treat rheumatism, spots, scurf and acne. Birch bark can be used as a diuretic, tonic, antiseptic and analgesic, and the leaves to treat cystitis. In a more abstract sense, being close to a birch reduces stress and strengthens our inner faith that we can be flexible and cope with change. It brings gladness.

Birch bark is potent when used as a magical parchment. Burnt as incense it clarifies the mind and uplifts the spirit. Broomsticks were traditionally made of birch twigs and miscreants were beaten with them, to drive out evil. Maypoles were made of birch, as was the Yule Log. Birch twigs also confer fertility, and were given to couples on their wedding night – after they had jumped the broomstick. The goddess Arianrhod, of the Silver Wheel of circumpolar stars, was

41

invoked, using birch, to aid fertility, birth and initiation. Although the Birch Moon ends some two weeks before the festival of Imbolc, at the start of February, there is much about the cleansing and creative qualities of the tree that correlates with the spirit of this feast at which priestesses were initiated and which is also called the Feast of the Poets. Birch conveys many caring qualities of the Feminine and can be used for protection, love and purification. Legend tells us to show special respect to the birch for, despite her delicacy and beauty, she becomes angry if trees are harmed or maligned near her. Who knows what subtle power resides in her spirit?

If birch is your birth moon you were born at a time when the power of light begins subtly, daily, to increase. You may be the 'new broom that sweeps clean'. You have resolve, faith in yourself and the ability to conceive new projects and 'earth' them in good soil. Your potential is tremendous and you possess clarity of purpose and possibly a visionary quality that enables you clearly to envision objectives and outcomes. Always be careful that your objectivity doesn't become clouded by a lack of realism and remember that being practical isn't the same as being realistic, for there are also subtle realities. Meditate on the qualities and customs associated with the birch and seek out the presence of your tree, if you can, to develop your potential.

Luis – Rowan Moon

Latin name *Sorbus aucuparia*   **Family** *Rosaceae*
Other names   Witchwood, Mountain Ash, Lady of the Mountain, Quicken Tree, Quickbeam
Runes   Nyd/Nauthiz ᚾ ᚿ
Celtic symbol   The Green Dragon
Deities   Mercury, Odin, Thor, Bride/Brigantia
Other associations   The elements air and fire, protection against enchantment, guardian of the earth energies, healing, success, control, psychism, the energy of the sun.

Rowan grows up to 9 metres (10 feet) in height and may live up to 200 years. It is an especially beautiful tree because its branches rarely die, so it retains its graceful silhouette. Rowan tolerates poor soil, but likes light and high altitudes. It flowers in May, but is

especially attractive in autumn when covered with berries, like red beads. However, the **berries are poisonous**.

The wood of the rowan is very tough and was used to make ship's masts, bows, spindles and spinning wheels. Walking sticks made of rowan are said to confer protection on those out at night and rowan sticks can dowse the presence of underground metals. Rowan provides an astringent and antibiotic. Its presence is calming, balancing and enables us to find strength of purpose.

Rowan was regarded as the Tree of Life in ancient times. Considered to be a feminine tree, to the Ash's masculine, Norse myth tells that the first woman was born from the rowan and the first man from the ash. Rowan is reputed to have saved the life of the god Thor by bending over a swift river, in which he was drowning, enabling him to climb out. The rowan moon includes the festival of Imbolc, a festival associated especially with the goddess Bride, patroness of the arts, including spinning and weaving and associated with the fiery arrows of inspiration – links which are echoed in the craft uses of rowan. Bride wet-nursed the young sun-god, the Mabon. The druids used smoke from rowan fires to conjure spirits and incense made from the leaves and berries promotes visions and banishes negativity. Groves of rowan were valued for their oracular qualities. The poetic muse can be conjured by carrying rowan berries to where water meets land and meditating. Rowan is especially powerful near stone circles and ley lines, where it both protects the earth and is enhanced by the dragon-power that is a personification of earth energy. Irish legend tells many tales of dragons guarding the rowan tree.

If you were born in the rowan moon, you have the ability to develop visionary powers and the chances are your sense of yourself as a unique individual is strong. Often ahead of your time, you may appear detached but you can be passionate about your principles and something of a humanitarian crusader against prejudice and bigotry. On the track of the inspirational, your thoughts are usually crystal clear, free of pre-conditioning. Use the influence of rowan to strengthen your visions, but use also its balancing qualities to connect you with the warmth of human feelings and make your ideas relevant to the society in which you live.

NUINN – ASH MOON

Latin name *Fraxinus excelsior*   **Family** *Oleaceae*
Other names   Husbandry tree, Heder (Lincolnshire term), Sister, Granny, Venus of the Woods
Runes Aesc/Ansuz ᚠ ᛈ ᚪ
Celtic symbol   Sea-horse or Trident
Deities   Poseidon, Neptune, Odin, Mercury, Nemesis, Andrasteia, Thetis
Other associations   The Air and Water
elements, marriage of opposites, linking inner and outer worlds, mental clarity, 'New Age' energies.

The ash is strong and elastic, growing to heights of more than 42 metres (140 feet), often found in old fossil beds. Old ash trees display ridges that look like wave edges impressed on to the sand of beaches. This tree has great affinity for water and has many water-absorbing features, such as conduits, tiny hairs in the leaves and widely spreading roots. Ash is one of the last trees to leaf and country lore states 'If the ash leafs before the oak, we're in for a soak, if oak leafs before ash, we're in for a splash'. The deep roots of the ash enable it to withstand gales and to live for several hundred years. It seems to attract lightning – 'Ash courts a flash'.

Ash grows quickly, does not split when worked and is tough and pliable. Ash wood was used for oars, coracles, furniture-making, wagons and sometimes bows. The Vikings believed it gave special power to their ships. It smells sweet when burnt. Ash trunks were split and children passed through them for healing. Infusions of ash leaves are said to confer longevity and can also cure rheumatism and act as a laxative. The wood and seeds are also considered to have aphrodisiac qualities. Ash heals the split we may feel from the natural world, its latter masculine associations connecting with more ancient links with the mother goddess.

Many ancient cultures believed that human essence originated in the ash tree. The goddess of justice, Nemesis, carried an ash branch. Here we have the inexorable face of the goddess, also associated with

solar cycles and the death of the sun-god, and the ash was one of the guises of the Goddess, having also lunar associations and affiliation with the tides – Nemesis was daughter of old Oceanus, the sea-god. Within the heart of ash is the embodiment of the female seductive qualities. The most famous ash tree is the mythic World Tree, Yggdrasil, from whose branches Odin hung, to gain the secret of the runes. A serpent twines at the roots of Yggdrasil, signifying the power of the Feminine principle, while an eagle perches on the top, signifying the Masculine. Souls were born in its branches and the Spring of Fate arose at its foot. Thus it united many elements. Ash, for the Druids, was the tree that ushered return to the 'here and now' after the experience of the sacred grove. Druids made magical wands and symbols from the roots of the ash. Ash has great affinity for water and is associated with speed over water and land – to place an ash-leaf in your car or on your motor-cycle is a modern charm to bring you safely home. Witches 'flew' on ash-handled broomsticks. All the magical parts of the Vikings' craft were of ash, as was the spear of Odin. As the phallic maypole, ash represents solar celebrations and the cycle of life. Indeed, ash unites many elements, and is hard to define simply – as its roots extend, so does its mythology, changing its emphasis as human culture has evolved. Because of this it can be a unifying and enlightening influence.

If ash is your birth moon you may be rather an enigmatic character, with a dual aspect to your nature. You are not just able to see both sides, you may almost *be* both sides. Artistic and pragmatic, sensitive yet strangely detached, kind yet sometimes cruel, many nuances of human nature are contained within you. You may appear naive, but in reality it is almost impossible to shock you, for you have a deep understanding of the seamy side of humanity. Do not attempt to be 'consistent' for that could iron out your sensibilities. Your great gift is your ability for understanding and compassion, but you need to learn to moderate this in order to protect yourself. Meditating in the presence of ash will enable you to be practical and to maintain a unity even while appreciating diversity.

Fearn – Alder Moon

Latin name *Alnus glutinosa*   **Family** *Betulaceae*
Other names Aller, Howler
Rune Isa |
Celtic symbol Hawk or Pentacle
Deities Bran, Pan, Verdandi, Mars, King Arthur
Other associations The elements of Water and
Air, prophecy, divination, protection.

Alder grows on swampy ground, river banks and at the edge of the forest, close to birch and hazel. Usually a small tree, it may reach heights of 21 metres (68 feet) and live for over 140 years. Its delicate appearance conceals its immense strength. Below ground its roots enrich the soil with nitrogen and it creates beneficial shade for plants, and fish in waters beneath it. After felling the white inner wood slowly turns pinky-red and appears to bleed. Because of this resemblance to humans the alder was held to be sacred. Alder Moon encompasses the Spring Equinox, when the growth of the fertility of the world is celebrated as light becomes stronger than darkness.

Alder wood does not decay in water and is used to make bridges and jetties. Dye of faery green comes from its flowers and red dye from the bark. Alder leaves were used by our ancestors to soothe tired feet and a decoction of alder bark can ease inflammation when bathed in. Alder aids in more subtle ways by healing a sad heart and enabling us to find a way, over and through the waters of our emotions, to a place of peace.

Irish legend tells how the first man was made from alder and the first woman from rowan. Alder is linked with the Welsh god-giant Bran, whose sister Branwen married the Irish lord Mattholoch. Trouble was caused between the Irish and Welsh by Bran's envious half-brother Evnissien, and Bran had to give the Irish his magic cauldron, that restored life to the dead, in order to appease them. However, Branwen was ill-treated and Bran invaded Ireland, using his great body to form a bridge over the river Shannon so the Welsh could pursue their foe – and thus linking with the bridge-making qualities of the alder. At length the Welsh were victorious, but only

seven remained alive with Bran mortally wounded by a poisoned arrow in the foot. However, Bran's head remained alive, with oracular powers. It was buried in the White Hill of London facing France, from where it was said the next invasion would arrive. Bran's sacred oracular birds, the ravens, still inhabit the Tower of London and it is said that Britain will not fall as long as they remain. Bran was also called Bran the Blessed, his beneficent qualities echoing those of the alder and alder wood was used by the Druids to make magic whistles to conjure Air elementals, so linking with the prophetic qualities of the god, as alder's leaf-buds of royal purple are also Bran's colour. The highest branch of the alder was known as the oracular singing head of Bran.

There is a heroic quality to individuals born in the Alder Moon and you will make your own way in life as a leader and pioneer. You rarely lack courage but you can be restless and impatient and you do not always perceive pitfalls in your paths. Generally you have energy and confidence and while you rarely rely on another to fight your battles, you are a loyal and protective friend to those you care for. Committed and sincere though you generally are, you do not always stop to think or to cultivate wisdom and circumspection. Meditate on the qualities of alder and seek out the presence of the tree to help you achieve far-sightedness and vibrancy of the spirit and to conjure into being the perceptive qualities that will enhance your enterprise.

SAILLE – WILLOW MOON

Latin name *Salix spp.*   **Family** *Salicaceae*
Other names Witches' aspirin, osier, pussy willow, Sally, withy, Tree of Enchantment
Rune Laguz ᚾ
Celtic symbol The Sea Serpent
Deities Hecate, Persephone, Kuan Yin, Selene, Circe, Cerridwen, Belili/Bel, Diana, Orpheus
Other associations The element of Water, the moon, dowsing, psychic abilities, magic, love, healing, fertility, protection.

Willows are familiar at watersides. The white willow is the largest of the many species, which include crack willow, weeping, bay, almond, purple and goat willow (the proper 'pussy willow'), among others. The supple twigs tend to droop and the leaves are long and slim. Willow twigs propagate easily, needing only to be placed in the ground to take root. Because its branches are pliable and strong, willow is used to make baskets and the trees are often 'pollarded' – cut off at shoulder height – to produce a mass of growth for this purpose. Willow was also used for boats and coracles. Aspirin derives from the willow. A drink made from the bark can ease rheumatism and decoctions can help relieve diarrhoea. The leaves and bark can be used in incense for healing spells. Sandalwood and willow can be burnt together, as the moon wanes, to conjure spirits. The presence of willow is deeply soothing, easing away discontent and raw emotions such as jealousy, self-pity and burning resentment.

When Orpheus journeyed into the Underworld to rescue his lost wife Eurydice, he carried willow branches on his travels. The magical power of his music was so haunting that trees and rocks moved to be close to him. The sound of wind in the willow tree is a powerful inspiration to poets. Persephone, Queen of the Underworld, had a sacred grove of willow and Circe planted a cemetery of willow for her rites of the moon. The ancient Sumerian goddess Belili was associated especially with the willow. She was later superseded by Bel/Belin, a solar god, but the feast of Beltane on or around 1 May honours the fertility, supreme enchantment and life-giving qualities of the Goddess. Hecate, the witch-goddess par excellence, was one of few ancient deities to survive in the pantheon of the Hellenic Greeks. Cross roads were sacred to her and the dread spirits of the night obeyed her commands. The dark moon is especially Hecate's time, when the Goddess is powerful but unseen, and terrifying to those who do not understand Her. Willow has a darker side, inexorable as the tides and the laws of life and death, and willows were often planted on graves in an echo of Celtic practice. Indeed, willow is the most magical of trees, surrounded by the mists of Otherworld.

If you were born in the Willow Moon you are close to the essence of nature. In a sense the primeval magic of the earth is in your bones, but it is unlikely that you are a noticeably mystical person, for you may well take the instinctual for granted. You have staying power, Mother Wit and are pragmatic enough not to miss chances.

Generally your memory is good and you may have access to what we may call 'race memory'. You may be stubborn, moody and find it hard, at times, to express how you feel. If hurt, you may feel this deeply. Use the energies of willow to reconnect to the rhythms of the earth, enable you to adjust and soothe you when you feel unsettled.

huathe – hawthorn moon

Latin name   *Crataegus monogyna*   **Family**   *Rosaceae*
Other names   Whitethorn, May, Bread and Cheese tree
Rune   Thorn/Thurisaz   ▷
Celtic symbol   The chalice
Deities   Vulcan, Hephaestus, Govannon,
Thor, Mars, Blodeuwedd, Olwen, Hera
Other associations   The elements of Fire and
Earth, access to Otherworld, fertility, guardian, cleansing, fulfilment.

Although hawthorn can grow to 10 metres (33 feet) in height it is more usually found in smaller form, as part of hedgerows, where it appears to adapt naturally to its position as a protective barrier – the thorns are actually stunted shoots. It is much associated with traditional English village life and with pagan nature festivities. Hawthorn has been with us for over 8,000 years, has been found in megalithic tombs and individual trees can live for more than 400 years. The trees will sometimes flower twice in a year. Common hawthorn is covered in white blossom as spring advances, signifying the bridal gown of the Goddess.

Hawthorn trees are small and so their wood is generally used for small items such as knife handles. The wood was believed to bring good luck. This wood burns readily and at a high heat. Haw berries can be made into wine or jelly. Folk wisdom says that hawthorns are safe to shelter beneath during thunderstorms. Hawthorn leaves are believed to be as nourishing as bread and cheese and it contains chemicals which are anti-spasmodic and diuretic – it is used with digitalis to treat heart problems. It is also good for palpitations, menopausal and circulatory problems. Hawthorns often grow by wells and sick children were carried to them for healing and wish-rags tied upon the tree. Hawthorn can cleanse and protect. It is

49

especially effective in healing sexual energies. This tree was highly prized and it was said that a high price would be paid by anyone needlessly felling one.

A well-known legend about the hawthorn concerns the staff of Joseph of Arimathea, which rooted upon Wearyall Hill near Glastonbury, so bringing the new Christian faith to Britain. This tree was said to be still living at the time of the English Civil War. A blossoming twig from the Glastonbury Thorn is still sent to the Queen at Christmas. After the crown of Richard III rolled under a bush in Bosworth Field, the Tudors claimed the hawthorn as their badge. Hawthorn is especially sacred to the Welsh sun-goddess Olwen, complement to Arianrhod of the silver wheel. Golden-haired Olwen was 'the white lady of the day' and the 'golden wheel of summer'. Where she trod she left white footprints of hawthorn and her father, Yspaddaden Pencawr was 'Giant Hawthorn'. Thirteen tasks (or, in some versions three by thirteen, i.e. thirty-nine) were demanded of her suitor, Culhwych, before he could marry her and overthrow the power of the hawthorn. The number thirteen, as we know, has lunar associations, and this may be a metaphor for the solar, usually thought of as masculine power, overcoming that of the moon. A preferable meaning is that in hawthorn, with all its associations with warmth, fertility and sexual joy, the sacred marriage of female and male takes place.

If hawthorn is your birth moon it is likely that you are filled with new ideas and creativity. Your talents and abilities are many and varied and you are resourceful and positive in coping with life. You may be a good strategist, sensing the vulnerable points of anyone who opposes you. Generally your nature is sensual and you may well be artistic and able to act, sing or perform in some way. You may need to be careful that you are not too impulsive and although your responses may be enthusiastic, you may not always be constant in relationships. Use the essence of hawthorn to ground you and to cleanse you, to enable you to use your gifts with energy and practicality and to open your vision. Hawthorn can also help you to find a depth and fulfilment in your sensuality that will enrich and steady your relationships.

ÐUIR – OAK MOON

Latin name   *Quercus robur*   **Family**   *Fagaceae*
Other names   Jove's Nuts, Father of Trees, King of the Forest
Runes   Tyr/Teiwaz ↑   Rad/Raido ᚱ   Ger/Jera ⟩ ᚦ ⟩
Eh/Ehwaz ⟨
Celtic symbol   White Horse or Golden Wheel
Deities   Zeus, Jupiter, Taranis, Thor, Juno,
Cybele, Balder, Esus, Diana, Rhea, Athene, Bride,
Demeter, Blodeuwedd, Dagda, Herne, Jehovah; any
sovereign deity
Other associations   The elements of Fire, Earth and sometimes
Air. Entrance to mysteries, keeper of mysteries, health, courage,
strength, inner spiritual resource, protection.

The oak is a majestic tree which is very long-lived. There are over
400 species of oak. This tree may live to be over 700 years old.
Acorns are food to a myriad of creatures and are an old fertility
symbol. Oak roots penetrate deep into the earth and the tree is very
durable. At one time England was covered in forest of oak, and the
tree has come to be synonymous with the stout hearts of the
countrymen and the mysteries of the earth itself. Duir, the ogham for
oak, was probably the origin of the term druid. Oak Moon spans the
time of the Summer Solstice – the triumphant peak of Nature, but
also the beginning of the growth of darkness. Thus joy, strength and
depth are associated with this tree.

Oak wood lasts for centuries. Being both strong and beautiful, it has
long been popular for use in buildings and furniture. Vikings made
their ships from oak and most of their weapons which were
associated with the god Thor, especially hammers, whose tree the
oak became. Oaks were used for ships down through history,
notably in the fleet that defeated the Armada, leading to the
statement by Philip of Spain that he would destroy every tree in the
Forest of Dean. Many oaks were replanted at the behest of Nelson,
after they had been felled to build ships. Oak bark is used as an
antiseptic tonic and astringent. Bruised leaves can be placed on
wounds to ease inflammation. Acorns have long been considered

especially lucky, preserving youth and bestowing longevity. The galls, or 'oak apples' formed by wasp larvae on oak twigs contain much of the tree-essence and were used to treat diarrhoea, or gargled for sore throats. The presence of oak helps to hearten the discouraged and fearful, encourages perseverance, promotes a positive attitude in people who are ill, gives focus, calm and ease. Of all the trees it is perhaps the most magical and powerful of the Otherworld portals, while its beams are favoured to make ordinary doors.

All over the world the oak has been considered a powerful and godlike tree, associated with many deities and festivities. It is a symbol of welcome and strength. Oak featured in sacred groves where the earth goddess imparted her wisdom, but she was superseded by male deities, who then spoke through the oak. As the oak is struck frequently by lightning it was associated with thunder gods such as Zeus and Thor. The Argo, ship of Jason, stealer of the Golden Fleece, was made of oak and had an oracular beam in the prow that warned of danger. The followers of Dionysus, the god of wine and ecstasy, the Maenads, were saved from retribution for their destructive actions by being turned into oak trees, so although the oak is associated with steadiness and safety there is an oblique connection with the ecstatic. The fires of the goddess Bride, later called St Bridget, were kept alight by acorns and some traditions define oak as the wood for the Yule Log. Both of these mythological connections link oak with the solar cycle and enduring life. Oak featured in the festivities at all the eight traditional festivals of the pagan world. King Arthur's round table was reputed to have been made of oak and Merlin is said to have inhabited an oak grove. The oak has shielded many a king or hero – real and mythical – including Charles II and Robin Hood, and it is also associated with Herne and Hunter, an aspect of the horned god of Nature. To the druids oak was especially sacred, for when the English oak played host to the mistletoe – a rare occurrence – the mistle-berries were seen as the semen of the God come to fertilise the Earth and thus the Sacred Marriage was seen to take place within its branches. Oak brings security and unity.

If oak is your birth moon then you are blessed with a broad vision and an optimistic, buoyant personality. Positive and truthful, you may be something of a risk taker, because you always believe that

the best will happen – and often it does! You probably have leadership qualities and a streak of nobility. You are generous, have good survival instincts, but you may be indiscrete and make commitments that cannot be fulfilled – you may also give too much of yourself. Use the spirit of oak to ground you deep within the earth and to connect you with the Otherworld realms, showing you how best to use your energies and where to commit yourself. Oak can give you steadiness and depth, and enhance your joyfulness.

TINNE – HOLLY MOON

Latin name *Ilex aquifolium*   **Family** *Aquifoliaceae*
Other names   Holme, hulm, holme chase, Hulver bush, Christ's thorn, Aunt Mary's Tree, Hollin, Poisonberry
Rune   Man/Mannaz ᛗ ᛉ
Celtic symbol   Flaming Spear and The Unicorn
Deities   Saturn, Hodur, Taranis, Thor, Mars
Others associations   The element of Fire, protection, dream magic, the hidden side of the God, courage, clarity of mind and wisdom. Also linked to Midwinter, and the Goddess as Crone and Wisewoman.

Holly is usually more of a large evergreen shrub than a tree, gaining heights of 12 metres (40 feet) or more. Holly leaves seem to reflect light and this, combined with its bright berries, makes it a heartening tree in winter. Holly is very demanding on the surrounding soil. Male and female flowers grow on separate trees and the loveliest flowers appear in summer – hence holly is associated with both summer and winter, for in winter its berries are resplendent and the rich greenery of the leaves is a reminder of vitality when all is barren. Holly is a very ancient dweller of the primeval forests.

Holly is used to make walking sticks, chessmen, printing blocks, handles, sills and to inlay furniture. Holly wood burns very hot and so was used by blacksmiths, who were themselves considered magical because of the changes they wrought in metal. It was also used for knife handles and, if the wood was unstained, this may have links with the 'white-handled knife' traditionally used by witches for practical tasks such as cutting herbs. In this holly's ancient, protective powers would have been operative. Holly can be used in incense to consecrate magical tools. Holly berries are poisonous, but an infusion of the leaves can treat catarrh, 'flu, pneumonia, rheumatism and fever. The presence of holly acts as a guardian and, if we meditate with this tree, holly can warn us or encourage us about a course of action. Holly teaches responsibility and helps those who feel resentful, jealous, bitter, irritable or oversensitive. The staunch, seasoned holly cures many ills.

Holly is said to shelter the people of Faerie and it was and is especially sacred at the Winter Solstice, offering protection to the newly-born sun-god. Here holly is something of a midwife, ushering in new life. However, holly's associations are also masculine – the spikes on the berries are likened both to the rays of the sun and to phallic shapes. Regarded by the Druids as lucky and protective, holly is synonymous with the tenacity of the natural world. Symbolic of new life but also of endurance, it was said to have sprung from beneath Christ's feet as he walked and is one of several woods from which the cross is said to have been made. This tree has the most primeval of associations, linked to the Wildman and the sexual energies that infuse the forest and all the manifest world. Notably, holly represents the dark aspect of the God, who battles with His light twin at Midsummer and wins the stewardship of the Waning Year from Oak King, who presides over the year as it waxes. Much of holly's qualities are appropriate for winter's depths, but the tree calendar presages the approach of winter by placing holly after oak and the Summer Solstice and covering the sacrificial harvest time of Lammas/Lughnasadh, when the Corn Spirit is cut down. Holly gives us the strength to face the coming darkness. Branches should not be cut from holly, but pulled, as befits a sacred tree. It is considered lucky for men to carry holly.

If holly is your birth moon you may well be cautious and circumspect, protective of yourself and others. Generally you are reliable, down-to-earth and tenacious and you can be supportive. You have the propensity to dream and the strength to turn dreams to reality. Probably you have a strong sense of roots and family – both personal and collective – and through this you can find a profound connection with the spirit of the earth. At times you may be over-sensitive and

'prickly' and may protect yourself by becoming something of a hermit or by taking on too much in the belief that you can, or should, cope. Use holly to protect you on all levels, including from your own unreasonable expectations. Let holly drive out any negative whisperings of your subconscious and fill you with hope and cheer.

COLL – HAZEL MOON

Latin name   *Coryllus avellana*   **Family** *Betulaceae*
Other names   Cobnut, Poet's tree, 'The helmeted one'
Celtic symbol   The Rainbow Salmon
Deities   Mercury, Hermes, Woden,
Fionn mac Cumhal, Thor, Aengus
Other associations   The elements of Water
and Air, dowsing, divination, intuition, finding the
hidden and acquiring wisdom, developing individuality.

Hazel can be a large shrub or small tree. It can reach 18 metres (60 feet) in height but is more likely to be nearer 6 metres (20 feet). Hazel loves damp places and grows near pools and rivers, but it bears more fruit if the land is well drained. Leafy frills around the hazelnut gave it its name of 'helmeted'. Hazelnuts can become petrified and keep for thousands of years and have been found in boglands, appearing like pieces of jet.

Hazels are often coppiced – cut off at ground level – in order to produce useful, elastic stems of small timber. Hazel is used for items such as clothes props, bean-poles, hedge stakes, basket-making, hoops and many others. It has also been used to build coracles and hazel twigs are used in dowsing. Hazels were regarded as bearing immortality and the hazelnut, as a repository of wisdom, was a powerful charm and a bringer of health of all kinds. The presence of hazel can bring the intuitive lightning-flash of vision. It has a light, bright atmosphere that inspires. Hazel doesn't 'pull punches' and for deeply emotional matters a gentler tree might be sought. The gift of hazel is a breath-taking clarity.

The hazel was revered by the Celts as a faerie tree of great knowledge and the Druids carried hazel rods for inspiration, possibly also using them as 'talking sticks'. Irish lore tells of Connla's Well, around which grew the nine hazels of wisdom – nine is a number associated with the Triple Goddess in the three times three and nine is also considered to be a number esoterically linked to the moon. So there are links with the Goddess as Sophia – divine wisdom – in this tree which possesses many characteristics that are also masculine. In Connla's Well swum the salmon of wisdom, who ate the hazelnuts that fell from the magical trees. Legend tells how Fionn mac Cumhal, the cunning hero of many adventures, came to the well to learn all knowledge from the poet Finegas. As he roasted a salmon a drop of juice fell on his thumb and Fionn sucked it off, thereby illicitly gaining the gift of wisdom, in the tradition of the Trickster. Tales such as this suggest that true knowledge is often come by suddenly, unexpectedly, in indirect ways and not by learning by rote. It is also said that the salmon achieved mystical knowledge. After two years journeying this fish finds its way upstream to the ancestral spawning grounds, so epitomising wisdom, respect for ancestry, the theme of rebirth and echoing human cycles. The salmon finds its place of origin. Salmons leap upstream, and the hazel is associated with speed in air and water. The association of hazel with air and flight has echoes of spirit flight undergone by shamans.

If hazel is your birth moon it is likely that you are quick-thinking, perspicacious and clever, with the gift of self-expression. Probably you are good at organisation, seeking to know all the details of a matter. You are inquisitive and, while this may sometimes lead you to pry a little, you have also the gift of teaching what you have learnt to others. Use hazel to deepen your knowledge to wisdom and to enable you to use what you know creatively. Hazel can also help if you are over-sensitive or critical by lifting you to higher, more panoramic perspectives. Seek the relaxation that will give wings to your intuition and guard against the over-cerebral or unnecessarily detailed.

MUINN – VINE MOON

Latin name *Vitis vinifera*   **Family** *Vitis spp.*
Celtic symbol   The White Swan
Deities   Venus, Branwen, Aphrodite,
Etain, Dionysus, Bacchus, Tammuz, Apollo, Osiris

Other associations   The element of Water, fecundity, dying and resurrecting gods.

The grape is one of the oldest fruits grown by humans and wine has been made from it for millennia. Records show that vines were cultivated in Egypt as long as 6,000 years ago, and grapeseed have been found in prehistoric tombs. All grapes will produce wine if fermented, but only certain climatic conditions will give good wine. Vines were probably first cultivated around the Caspian Sea and over the last 300 years they have been introduced to Australia, South Africa and America. Vines can be trained or grown as bushes. Being deciduous they shed their leaves in winter. There are about eighty species of the genus – *Vitis vinifera* is the Old World wine. Vines can grow to a great age. The Great Vine in Hampton Court, near London, dates from 1768 and still bears fruit.

Vines are grown for wine, dessert grapes and raisins. Vines, with their intoxicating produce, are symbolic of joy and ecstasy. However, the true meaning of ecstasy is 'ex stasis' – moving away from the here and now in out-of-body experience. The vine relates to sensual experience but also to death and sacrifice, as the nature-god forms a sacrifice as the corn is cut. Thus vine is connected to the deepest rhythms and the most potent instinctual and physical experiences. In vine we see something of the embodiment of the pagan path which seeks to find transcendence, not by denying the body, but by more fully identifying with it and the mystical essence of nature. Vine can show us the way to pleasure and gratification, but it also teaches us that there is a season to all.

Dionysus is one of many embodiments of the sacrificial god. Son of Zeus, it was his mission to teach humans how to grow the vine. In carrying this out he had many adventures, in one of which he encountered a band of pirates who were determined to sell him as a slave. Dionysus was bound and placed in the hold, but after the ship had set sail vines began to grow all over the ship. Unease crept into the hearts of the sailors, turning to terror when the bonds fell from their captive and he turned into a mighty lion. The pirates leapt from him, into the sea, where they all became dolphins. Misfortune, as well as pleasure attend the gift of the vine and Dionysus is killed by the hero Perseus. While in the Underworld he buys his rebirth by the promised gift of his 'best beloved' which the dark lord Hades demands as a condition of his release. This 'best beloved' is the vine, which at the behest of the god now sprang up in the Underworld itself. Dionysus was now able to take his place with the other Immortals in Olympus. Being a plant both of darkness and light, the vine is associated with goddesses who were abducted and spent time in the Underworld, or with a husband/lover who represented the dark face of the God – for instance, Guinevere with Mordred, Etain with Midir in Irish legend. Vine Moon spans the Autumn Equinox, a strange and subtle time of changeover, hauntings and weather that may be unpredictable or with an ethereal quality of misty sunshine.

If vine is your birth moon you probably have a sensual streak and an instinctual knowledge of the earth, and yet you may appear very cool and self-possessed. You are capable of forward planning and may well be efficient and organised. You have the gift of creating harmony and balance and of bringing order and beauty into life. At your best you have indulgence and restraint in equal measure. Use the presence and aura of vine to keep your connection with the joys of life and to remind you of life's cyclicity in a way that enhances your appreciation of it. Vine can help you to let go of any tendency to be too controlling, so you may find peace and enjoyment.

GORT – IVY MOON

Latin name   *Hedera helix*   **Family**   *Arialaceae*
Rune   Ior   ᚼ
Celtic symbol   The Butterfly
Deities   Osiris, Dionysus, Bacchus, Saturn,
Persephone, Hecate, Ariadne, Rhiannon, Arianrhod
Other associations   The element of Water,
immortality, eternal love, the blessings of strength,
revelry, attachment, fidelity, the male trinity.

Ivy is a glossy evergreen, clinging to tree trunks and walls by means of small roots. It is bad for trees, but most attractive on walls. Its flowers bloom in autumn and are filled with nectar, so any bees that are still about are attracted to the plant. Although some of the lower branches of Hedera may trail along the ground, the plant can reach

to a height of 30 metres (99 feet). Ivy will grow into a tree, if permitted. **All parts of the plant are poisonous**.

Ivy can be used in the making of incense where Saturnian influences are required, to bind, ground and protect. Cups made of ivy were believed to cure children who had whooping cough and wine goblets were made from ivy. It was believed that drunkenness could be prevented by wreathing one's brow with ivy. Because ivy was sacred to Bacchus/Dionysus, the god of wine, the custom grew of hanging a bush of ivy outside an inn to announce the arrival of new wine – hence the saying 'a good wine needs no bush'. It was the chewing of ivy leaves that was said to provoke the frenzy of the priestesses of Bacchus. Ivy is carried by women for good luck. It can be bandaged on corns to ease them and the leaves, soaked in rosewater and placed on the temple, are a remedy for a stubborn headache. The presence of ivy teaches us constancy, steadfastness and faith in our ability to succeed. The armour of the Greeks and Romans was adorned with ivy and poets were crowned with ivy wreaths.

Ivy has connections with goddesses of the cosmic loom, such as Ariadne and Arianrhod of the Silver Wheel – the circumpolar stars, where the souls of the dead retreat to await reincarnation. Legend tells how Ariadne was spurned by her lover Theseus and rescued by Bacchus, who loved her dearly. When she died he was bereft, flinging her crown of ivy leaves into the sky, where it became the glittering constellation Ariadne's Crown or Corona Borealis. Ariadne then became immortal and was restored to Bacchus who, in his overwhelming joy, resumed his vocation of inspiring revelry and wine-making in humankind. So the evergreen significance of ivy is enshrined in the heavens. To the Celts ivy was associated with the portals of the Otherworld, the Faerie domain and the world of ancestral memory that the autumn evoked into consciousness.

If ivy is your birth moon it is likely that you have staying power and many talents that give you a unique and interesting personality. Radical and often artistic, you may have the ability to project an aura of success and confidence whatever your true circumstances. Both canny and generous, you can be manipulative at times and you may not always be decisive or constant. Rather than avoiding disputes, this can involve you in them. Use the presence of ivy to enhance your tenacity and to enable you to hold to your purpose, even if you decide to keep it to yourself. Ivy can inspire you to climb steadily and to 'hang in there' – it can also inspire you with faith and show you how to celebrate life.

NGETAL – REED MOON

Family name   *Gramineae*
Other names   Windlestraw, Goss
Celtic symbol   The Stone or the White Hound
Deities   Pluto, Persephone, Pan, Syrinx, Pwyll, Hecate, Hermes
Other associations   The elements of Water and Air, loss and transformation, hidden emotions, the written word, preservation, rebirth.

Although the reed is scarcely a tree, it is beautiful and graceful, growing sometimes to a height of over 3 metres (10 feet). Its roots grow deep and its leaves are bright green. Reeds grow almost all over the world, along the banks of lakes, in marsh ground and shallow waters, where reed swamps are often formed. The flowers are initially a purple-brown, hanging like plumes, from the summer into the autumn, when they fade to grey and produce long silky hairs that turn into a mass of down and carry the seeds into the wind.

Reed may be used for fencing, thatching and making furniture while the reed beds provide food and nesting places for birds. Reeds were also used in the first writing implements and so have a basic connection to this skill, which marked a change in the consciousness of humankind. The presence of the reed-spirit and the sound of the wind sighing in a reed-bed can enable us to let go of old patterns of behaviour and indeed of anything in life we need to move away from, and reed can show us a passage to a fresh start. Reed may also show us what is worth preserving, as thoughts can be 'preserved' and passed on through the generations in the written word.

The most well-known legend about the reed concerns Pan, the nature-god and the nymph Syrinx. Pan is one of the personifications of the Horned God who exemplifies the power of nature. The horns can be seen as phallic or as representing the lunar crescents – they are both a

salute to animal origins and a crown of divinity. Pan embodies the wild spirit of the natural world. When he falls in love with Syrinx, he pursues her, never dreaming that she does not, secretly, desire his embrace. Just as he is about to catch her she begs the gods to save her, which they accomplish by turning her into a reed-bed. As the arms of the god close over empty air all that stands before him is a clump of reeds, keening in the wind and Pan realises that what he loves has been irretrievably lost to him. Being a stout pragmatist, Pan adjusts. He plucks the reeds and makes from them the Pan-pipes, whose strange and haunting sound becomes his signature. Reed is also associated with Hermes, the only god who could come and go at will through the Underworld, acting as a psychopomp, or leader of souls. Hermes was also the god of communication. Reed is associated with all transformations and with the 'underworld' of emotions, as well as the abode of the dead – the swampy ground that reed inhabits is a metaphor for strong, deep feelings – the Celts believed that the penetrating roots of reed were associated with a hidden dryad, or tree-spirit. These feelings can be transmuted to positive action or used as a passage to knowledge. Reed moon encompasses the Celtic festival of Samhain, Feast of the Ancestors, when the powers of the hidden are honoured. For the Celts beginnings took place in the womb of darkness, day began at nightfall, the year began as autumn set in – thus Samhain/Hallowe'en is the Celtic New Year. Reed is thus sacred to the Hag aspect of the Goddess, she who destroys in order to bring renewal, the tomb that is also the womb.

If reed is your birth moon you are not likely to be a person of half-measures. Gutsy and often uncompromising, you are probably capable of facing what others shun, although you may keep quiet about it. You tend to generate a powerful personal field, and there may be dramas in your life – you are a passionate person. Capable of making radical changes, you may regenerate not only your own life but the fabric of existence more generally. You are a survivor and may evoke strong feelings in others, who will be either friends for life or enemies – by the same token you usually have powerful feelings about others. Expressing your feelings in poetry or art, or talking about them to a sympathetic and trustworthy confidante will aid you in integrating your emotions. Use the presence of reed to facilitate transformations in life, showing you the truth of your feelings and enabling you to move on, make changes or stand firm, as required. Reed can connect you with your strength and your deepest roots, translating the problematic into the poetic, enabling you to be creative and aiding in the alchemy of the spirit.

RUIS – ELDER MOON

Latin name   Sambucus nigra   **Family**   Caprifoliaceae
Other names   Bourtree, Lady Elder, Lady Ellhorn,
Old Lady, Old Sal, pipe tree, bole tree
Rune   Fehu/Feoh ᚠ
Celtic symbol   The Black Horse or The Raven
Deities   Venus, Hela, The Goddess as Crone, Cerridwen
Other associations   The elements of Earth and Water,
regeneration, female mysteries, the cauldron of rebirth,
menstruation.

Elder is so common in England that it is sometimes considered almost a weed. Most elders are large shrubs, no more than 9 metres (30 feet) in height, although old records suggest that elder trees with trunks 2 metres (6 feet) in diameter used to be found. Elder propagates very easily, simply from a broken twig placed in the soil. Part of the crazy charm of elder is its untidiness, caused by the many stems of the tree that grow upwards for a while and then bend over. Red sap oozes from the wood when cut, hence its link with menstruation. Elder flowers in June and has a musky scent, while in early autumn it is laden with blue-black berries. Elder produces a reserve bud beneath the main bud in case of frost damage, hence the association with earthy wisdom and regeneration.

The healing powers of elder are legion. The bark is a diuretic and purgative, the shoots clear the chest, the flowers are mildly analgesic and can be used to alleviate catarrh, bronchitis, rheumatism, colds and fevers, conjunctivitis, chilblains, constipation and other ills. Elder wood was used for fishing rods, mathematical instruments, tool handles, spoons, adult toys and shoemakers' pegs. Hollow elder twigs can be made into whistles – flutes made from the tree were said to summon spirits, and an old stringed musical instrument

called a sackbut was made from the wood. The presence of elder is grounding, bringing the ancient wisdom of the earth – true Mother Wit. Elder's counsel is pragmatic, unsentimental and basic, bearing the essence of the primeval soil.

Elder is a tree much associated with witchcraft and the pagan, feminine powers and as such has acquired a rather dubious reputation over the last two thousand years. Witches were said to turn into elder trees and it has the reputation for being the tree in which Judas hanged himself and having been used as the wood of the cross – although it does not lend itself to forming so large an object. Thus the tree has been given an evil aura, possibly because its many properties were made use of by the old wisewomen and healers. Elder is connected both with witchcraft and with charms against witches and is feared and revered. Some native Americans believe that elder is the mother of the human race. Gypsies consider it is bad luck to burn elder wood and that the elder mother will exact fearful revenge for such an act. Elder's unruly growth hints of the uncontrollable, unknowable aspect of nature and the black heart that beats within the earth, warning us to respect that to which we owe our existence. Elder grows from the Underworld into the here and now and is the tree of the Dark Queen. Elder Moon takes us past the Winter Solstice and through the very trough of the year with all its mysteries of death and rebirth.

If elder is your birth moon it may take you some years to grow into the capacity to develop the depth of wisdom that can be yours. You need to get to know things profoundly and your mind is generally far-ranging. Meanings and deep significance are important to you, but you can also have a happy-go-lucky, carefree side. You tend to 'tell it like it is' and to assume that good fortune will be yours, which is often the case! Adventurous and impulsive, you may appear to live for the moment, but you are truly aware that all we do has significance and consequence. Sometimes you can be unreliable or over-casual and you may go off at a tangent. Use the presence of elder as a grounding, centring influence, to keep you on the right track and to give relevance to your speculations. Elder can keep you switched into the wisdom of the Ancestors and empower your dreams and visions.

100 – The yew tree

Latin name *Taxus baccata*   **Family** *Taxaceae*
Rune Eolh/Eihwaz   ↑
Deities Hecate, Saturn, Banbha
Other associations The element of Earth, the door of rebirth, rest between lives, divination, dowsing, bow-making, the ancestors.

In the tree calendar, yew is not associated with a month but with the Nameless Day, 23 December, which is contained within the Elder Moon. Thus yew cannot be considered as a birth moon, but it has profound links with the trough of the year and so it is fitting to consider it as part of the tree calendar. The Nameless Day is an intercalary day – the result of the division of 365 by 13, which gives 28 and an odd day, incorporated into Elder Moon. However, it seems appropriate that an extra tree be attached to the magical time of the Winter Solstice, when chaos reigns for a short space, all is broken down and reborn, as the face of the Goddess changes from Crone to Mother and Maiden and she gives rebirth to the sun-god and, in a sense, to Herself. 23 December corresponds with that breathless time just before the sun is seen definitely to be moving closer in the sky, for 'Solstice' means 'standing still of the sun'. After the Nameless Day the movement of the sun is established and the birth of the sun-god has taken place. To my mind, this entire week is of great significance, and I would associate yew with the approximate period of 19–25 December.

Yew is an evergreen, from the primeval forests that reigned before broadleaved trees appeared. It has an immense lifespan, living for over 1,000 years and one yew tree, the Fortingall Yew, in Perthshire, is reputed to be 9,000 years old. The reason for the great age of the yew is its habit of rooting its branches, which then grow in the earth, giving yew its connection with life after death and rebirth. Yew is often found in churchyards and can reach heights of 23 metres (75 feet) – yews are believed to reach their roots into the mouths of corpses. Male and female flowers appear on separate trees and yew pollen can cover large areas with its golden dust.

Yews were used for the famous English crossbow and, when the armies gathered outside churches to be blessed, the archers made their bows from the trees that grew there – it is said that kings ordered the planting of yews specifically for that purpose. This wood is very hard, used for fences, wine barrels, furniture and ship-masts – it is extremely strong and durable, resistant to decay and burns at a very high heat. Yew sticks were cast as a form of divination by the Celts, and yew posts were used for Ogham scripts. **Yew is extremely poisonous** and the word 'toxin' derives from yew's Latin name. However, recent discoveries indicate that yew may contain an anti-cancer drug. While this is exciting it puts the yew tree in jeopardy as bark is stripped from very ancient trees to obtain the substance that could be obtained, at slightly greater cost, from the leaves. British yews need preservation orders to avert the possibility – all too common – of humans biting the hand that feeds them. Yew contains unfathomable wisdom and is a store of ancestral knowledge as well as a door to future generations. Yew can help us to gain a sense of perspective when we are harried by minor concerns, for it plugs us in to the eternal, to the heart of the earth and the inter-galactic void where new constellations are birthed. Yew can connect us to loved ones who have passed on.

Many stories tell of yews growing on the graves of lovers. The lovers from Irish legend, Deirdre and Naoise, were united even in death as yew tree branches entwined over their graves. A similar story is told of Tristan and Iseult. Legend tells how, in days when the world was young, the yew tree pined for brighter foliage, so the faeries gave it leaves of gold. The yew was happy, but robbers stripped it bare, leaving it bereft. So the faeries consoled it with leaves of pure crystal and the yew rejoiced. But a storm of hail arrived and all the crystals shattered. So the yew was given green leaves, but these were eaten by animals. Thereafter the yew was content with its dark clothing, realising it was safer and more durable than prettier leaves, and so the yew found comfort and ease. Yew was one of the trees to be decorated with sparkling objects at Yule, to encourage the return of light, a custom which evolved into the Christmas tree. Like all evergreens, it is an ever-present promise of resurgent life.

PRACTICE

This completes our look at the tree calendar and in all probability you have identified your own tree and have been thinking what it means for you. However, all trees can have meanings for us or can interact with us in ways we find meaningful. Do not confine yourself to your birth moon tree, but see what others have to offer you, in thinking about the mythology concerned or by seeking out the presence of the tree, meditating and experiencing its effect – for all trees have their message, of peace, beauty and wisdom, for anyone who sincerely seeks. In addition, the thirteen tree moons do correspond with the 360 degrees of the zodiac, which in this case is divided into thirteen, not twelve, as with the zodiacal signs. This means that if the tree moons were plotted for you on your astrological birth chart, you would have planets, Ascendant (sign on the eastern horizon at birth) and Midheaven in several different 'trees' – so go by the trees you feel an affinity with, not just your birth moon tree, and let them expand your spirit.

4

A SELECTION
OF TREES

Oh, I who long to grow;
I look outside myself, and the tree
inside me grows

Rainer Maria Rilke

ACACIA

Acacia spp.
Deities   Ra and Solar Deities,
Astarte, Osiris, Diana
Other associations   The element of Air,
rebirth, initiation, immortality.

There are some 800 varieties of acacia, including wattle, the national emblem of Australia. The wood is used in incense, combined with sandalwood, when it promotes psychic powers. It bears both white and red flowers, and is said to have been the plant that formed Christ's crown of thorns.

The Hebrews regarded acacia as the wood of the Tabernacle and it was therefore sacred. The thorns of the plant represent the lunar crescent. The white and red flowers signify life and death, and death and rebirth. This tree was also associated with Egyptian sky-goddess Neith, weaver of the cosmic loom. Because of its lunar connections acacia has links with all aspects of life, from innocence to the wordless wisdom of the initiate, reminding us that in life there is death and in death, life.

The mature seeds of *acacia aneura* also called 'mulga' are an important food source for the Australian Aborigines. A traditional form of preparing them, taken from *Punu-yankunytjatjara Plant Use: Traditional Methods of Preparing Foods, Medicines, Untensils and Weapons from Native Plants*, compiled and edited by Cliff Goddard and Arpad Kalotas, Institute for Aboriginal Development, 1985–8 (Angus & Robertson), is as follows:

1 You put some mulga branches on an old flat termite nest and leave them there.
2 Then after a while, after travelling around a bit, come back and check it. It dries out.
3 'Ah! This food of mine has dried out nicely!' Then you thresh it.
4 As you thresh it, the pods fall out all over the place.
5 By rubbing them and tapping them you get the seed out, and put it in a wira dish.
6 Then you yandy the mulga seed in the wira dish.
7 Once it's yandied, you tip the clean seed into mimpu bowls.
8 Then load up on your head and return to camp.
9 Having brought it to camp, you parch the seeds in hot ashes, and the hard seed cases crack open.
10 After roasting it, you winnow and yandy it again, to separate the seed inside.
11 Then you get a grindstone, and grind it up, licking it as you grind.
12 You put a collecting vessel beneath the lower grindstone and it builds up in that.
13 We used to eat it as kids. We'd get full.

14 It's an important food: a food of our grandfathers and grandmothers, a strong food. We grew up on this food, without flour.

Mulga is a tree that typifies the vast, dry inland; it is found right across Australia. It is distinctive because of its attractive silver-grey foliage, which points upwards, to avoid the direct rays of the searing sun. To survive in drought it drops many of its leaves. When rain falls once more it is channelled down the slanting branches to enter the soil where the roots can suck it up. It flourishes in areas receiving as little as 200 mm (8 inches) of rain a year, and its branches can be used as fodder, felled in great numbers by gangs from large sheep stations, to keep sheep alive in the great drought at the turn of the twentieth century. Mulga wood is used extensively to make ornaments. The Aborigines made great use of it, for boomerangs, spears, digging sticks, clubs and shields. The word 'mulga' itself comes from an Aboriginal word for a long, narrow shield.

apple

Pyrus malus
Ogham   Quert
Rune   Ing   ᚷ
Deities   Aphrodite, Venus, Freya, Pomona, Olwen, Shekinah, Ishtar, Cerridwen, Nemesis
Other associations   The element of Water, love, healing, foundation, destiny, inspiration.

Different species were grafted on to the crab apple tree, indigenous to Britain, in order to produce the fruit tree we now have, classified as *malus domestica*. Cider apples are the closest kin to the crab. Old apple trees are the commonest of all trees to host the mistletoe. The apple blooms in mid to late spring and its flowers have a heady, sweet aroma. The uses of apple are legion and it has many therapeutic qualities that are good for infections, constipation, rheumatism, anaemia, bronchitis and many other conditions. Meditating in the presence of apple trees encourages love and trust and a blossoming of the heart so that we may accept ourselves and open out towards other people. Because of its links with sensual delights, the apple came to be mistakenly demonised by dogmas that disliked the body and so appeared in stories as sinister and representative of wickedness as in the story of Snow White and the poisoned apple.

The druids pay especial homage to the apple tree, because it most commonly carries the mistletoe. Apple has long been considered the food of the gods and the faerie folk – it is associated with the Underworld and brings a sense of fellowship at the autumn festival of Samhain/Hallowe'en. Apple boughs were the charm that enabled heroes to return from the Underworld. Ancient paradises were generally orchards, the Greek example being the Garden of the Hesperides, located in the western seas where the sun sank daily. Here there was a sacred apple tree that conferred immortality. A parallel Celtic legend tells of the Isles of the Blessed, where the Tree of Knowledge grew with its three scared apples – this tree was guarded by the goddess Cerridwen in the guise of a serpent. The symbolism of the apple is complex. Our sexual drives can connect us to our 'underworld' and sexual love is a transformative act that can mean a type of 'death' – however, true love is said to conquer all, even death. The myth of the judgement of Paris is well known – Paris, prince of Troy, had to decide which of the three goddesses, Hera, Athene or Aphrodite was the most beautiful. He chose Aphrodite, giving her an apple as a sign, whereupon she awarded him with the love of the most beautiful woman alive – Helen of Troy, but Helen was already married to Prince Menelaus and so began the Trojan wars. Apple is a poignant reminder of the power of love, how essential it is to life, of its magic, is link with destiny – and its beauty.

BEECH

Fagus sylvaticus
Ogham Phagos
Rune Nauthiz ⌐ ⌐
Deities Saturn, Zeus
Other associations The elements of Air, Fire – and possibly Earth, old writings, the recovery of ancient wisdom, prosperity, divination, wishes, letting go of rigid ideas.

Beech trees form lovely shady woods, lending themselves especially to rituals due to the ground space and seclusion offered. Beech bark is susceptible to light, but when the trees are grouped and there is plenty of shade the lower branches are shed. The silvery trunks and the chant of the wind in the leaves gives a magical atmosphere. Beeches grow to about 42 metres (138 feet) high and are the most delicate and feminine of the larger trees. Beech makes beautiful parquet flooring and some articles of furniture. Beech tar has been used to treat eczema and other skin problems. Meditating in the presence of beech trees can be liberating, clearing to mind and emotions, enabling us to let go of tired habits and ideas that have been holding us back. Beech is also a means of connecting with our past and the wisdom offered thereby.

Beech is called 'The Mother of the Woods' – the beech queen beside the oak king. Beech wood is reputed to be the first prepared surface on which words were written and as words have a powerful effect on human consciousness this itself is, in a sense, magical. Because of this, beech connects to all the gods of wisdom and writing such as Odin, Hermes, Thoth, Ogma/Ogmios the Celtic god who invented the Ogham script and warrior of the Tuatha de Danaan faerie Irish people. A wish can be written on beech and buried – as the wood returns to the earth, so the wish will manifest. Because of its connection with the passage of time, through writing, beech is linked to Saturn, Old Father Time himself. As the sun streams to earth in rays between beech trees, we see the meeting of earth and sky wrought by all trees, but perhaps especially by the beech. On the South Downs in Sussex there is a special clump of beech called Chanctonbury Ring, planted within a prehistoric bank and ditch about 200 years ago, and considered especially enchanting. It is reputed to be used for pagan ritual.

BLACKTHORN

Prunus spinosa
Ogham   Straif
Rune   Thorn/Thurisaz, Stan   ᚦ
Deities   The Crone aspect of the Goddess, Saturn, Mars, Thor
Other associations   The elements of Fire and Earth, cleansing, karma, barriers which can eventually be surmounted, curses, protection.

This is a knobbly little tree that often grows near hawthorn and can be mistaken for it. However blackthorn flowers earlier and the blooms have a musky, sensual aroma. The fruit are called sloes, which are black and bitter but can be made into sloe gin. Plum, greengage and damson may derive originally from this wild tree. Blackthorn wood is tough and was used to make the Irish shillelagh and staffs for staff fighting at village fairs. It is an excellent hedge-tree, forming an impenetrable barrier. Blackthorn can help us to cast out negativity and keep it at bay and it can help us burst through painful emotions. While this is not precisely soothing, a storm of tears in the presence of blackthorn can be therapeutic, helping acceptance and helping us to move on.

Blackthorn is associated with the Dark Goddess and it was thought most unlucky. However, this aspect of the Goddess devours only to give new life. To followers of the Old Religion both darkness and light are acceptable and so the gifts of blackthorn, while not perhaps gentle, are valued. However, in a dogmatic religious climate, blackthorn became associated with evil and was added to the witches' pyres – this was a final irony as the wood was believed to be used in evil magic. One origin of the 'devil's mark' sought by witchfinders was that the devil pricked his followers with blackthorn thorns. Thorns were indeed used in unmagical ways to administer poison or to cause horses to bolt. The negative properties of the blackthorn are enshrined in the story of Sleeping Beauty, where she pricks her finger with a spindle and falls into a dead sleep. The castle is then surrounded by a thick hedge of black thorns, until the handsome prince arrives. Of course, this is all caused by the maligned third fairy, who is really the Crone aspect of the Triple Goddess, much denigrated and demonised. Tales like this hint that She may be vengeful (possibly as a result of being denied) – they also indicate that through the adversity which She may bring comes great joy, eventually, as Sleeping Beauty awakes to a magical romance that would not have been hers had her life been less turbulent. Blackthorn, with its heady blossom appearing in a winter landscape, reminds us that our sexuality is linked to our karma. This may not be always easy. As Kahlil Gibran writes in *The Prophet* (Heinemann, 1987): 'your pain is the breaking of the shell that

encloses your understanding' and 'your joy is your sorrow unmasked'. These ideas are appropriate to blackthorn.

BO

Ficus religiosa
Deities   Vishnu, Buddha, Jupiter
Other associations   The element of Air, meditation, enlightenment, protection, perfection.

This tree is also called pipul or bodhi tree. The god Vishnu and Buddha are reputed to have been born under a bodhi tree. This is the tree under which Buddha was meditating when he achieved the state of enlightenment. In India this tree is believed to be the source of Soma, the draught of immortality.

CEDAR

Cedrus libani
Deities   Tammuz and solar deities
Other associations   The element of Fire, purification, strength, incorruptibility, majesty.

Cedars are stately evergreens whose branches grow in flat tiers and whose cones are shaped like barrels. The cedar of Lebanon is the most famous, chosen by Solomon to build his temple. The timber is long-lasting and was used for palaces and boats. Many fragrant woods are known as cedar but not all are true cedars – the pencil cedar of the eastern USA is in fact a kind of juniper. Cedar is used in sweat lodges by native Americans and in incense to purify and induce visions, as in the 'Fire of Azrael' incense made famous by Dion Fortune in *The Sea Priestess* (Aquarian, 1989) which consisted of juniper, sandalwood and cedarwood. Cedar is used for chests and wardrobes because it is pleasantly scented and repels insects.

Sumerian myth tells how the hero Gilgamesh went into the cedar forest in search of glory, accompanied by his dear friend Enkidu. Aided by his mother, the goddess Ninsun and the sun god, Shamash, Gilgamesh went forth, despite portents of devastation.

Enkidu persuaded him to begin to retreat from the forest but he felled a tree and the guardian of the forest, the monstrous and fearsome Humbaba, approached. When Humbaba stood before him, huge and terrible, even Gilgamesh was afraid, but Shamash came to his aid with a great wind that placed Humbaba at the hero's mercy. Humbaba offered to serve Gilgamesh, but Enkidu advised him not to trust him so Gilgamesh slew the ancient and powerful keeper of the forest. Now Gilgamesh and Enkidu felled and cleared the forest and took the mighty head of Humbaba to lay before the creator god, Enlil. However, Enlil was outraged and demanded the life of the one who had persuaded Gilgamesh to kill Humbaba and uprooted the trees, so they could never more grow. So Gilgamesh, whose life had promised so much, lost his best friend and, despite his great deeds, eventually died in obscurity. The meaning of this myth seems clear – Gilgamesh goes to the forest for initiation, to overcome his fear and to grow mighty – in effect to develop his individuality and spiritual essence. But he becomes too vain and forgets the responsibilities that come with strength and that he has not accomplished his deeds without help. He does not value the forest or respect its power – he even kills Humbaba, spirit of Nature, the Wildman, the Green Man. Looking for the immortality that comes with spiritual awakening, he is distracted by the fame that can come with deeds of force. He cuts down the forest that held so much and in so doing he loses half of himself, his friend Enkidu, and eventually dies himself. This ancient tale from 5,000 years ago has such obvious metaphorical meanings for us today!

COOLIBAH

Eucalyptus coolabah
Deities   Eucalyptus may be associated
with the Moon and Saturn
Other associations   The element of Water, healing.

Coolibah is a well-known Australian tree, usually fairly small but sometimes reaching almost 20 metres (65 feet) where water is plentiful. It grows along watercourses and places liable to flooding, in most dry, inland Australian states. It has rough, box-like bark on the trunk and large branches while smaller branches tend to be white

and smooth. The wood is hard and heavy, good for fence posts. Pioneering bushmen used it for making wheels and shafts. 'Coolibah' is derived from the Aboriginal.

Like many Australian trees it has inspired songs, and was immortalised by Banjo Paterson's jolly swagman, camping beneath its branches, in 'Waltzing Matilda'. The tree called the DIG tree is a coolibah, growing on the bank of Coopers Creek. 'DIG' was scoured into the trunk to indicate a cache of stores left for the explorers Bourke and Wills, in 1864, and the old tree still stands, strong and healthy. Roger Oxley (see Futher Reading) writes:

> Coolibahs in themselves are not particularly spectacular. However, if you add the Paroo, a sunset, reflections on the water and a couple of cold stubbies, then you have all the ingredients of an idyllic setting.

CYPRESS

Cupressus macrocarpa
Rune   Ear   ᛦ
Deities   Hecate, Hades/Pluto
Other associations   Mourning and consolation, helpful in crisis to aid transition.

The cypress is a cone-bearing evergreen with fern-like sprays of branches. The Mediterranean cypress is seen in British churchyards, the Monterey cypress is planted as a hedge in Britain and Australia while the Lawson cypress is a magnificent timber tree in the USA. The great doors of St Peter's in Rome were made of cypress and lasted 1,000 years. Like cedar the wood smells sweet, is used for furniture and, as it lasts well in water, also for boats. Cypress consoles those whose loved ones have died, helping the mourning process so that an inner transformation can take place and a place of acceptance can be found, inwardly. Essential oil of cypress is good for coughs, haemorrhoids, varicose veins, diarrhoea and menstrual problems.

Cypress has many links with funerals, mourning and the departed. Sprigs of the wood were tossed into graves to help the deceased in the hereafter. However, the scent of cypress oil is gently soothing rather than gloomy. Legend tells how Orpheus had cypress as his constant companion. Orpheus knew the most poignant of losses, for he had won the freedom of his wife, Eurydice, on condition that he did not look to check she was following him until he reached the upper world again. Just as he was almost there, Orpheus could wait no longer – he stole a glance and Eurydice was lost to him forever. Thereafter Orpheus mourned endlessly, doing nothing except play music so enchanting that even the trees lifted up their roots and moved to be next to him. The cypress had itself once been a boy who, having killed a beautiful stag by accident, had pleaded with the gods to turn him into a tree so he could endlessly mourn the magnificent creature. Legends abound with accounts of humans turned into trees to escape from their fate or suffering. Trees offer a place of safety where we can make connection with the timeless and where we can rediscover innocence.

ELM

Ulmus campestris
Ogham Ailm
Rune Gebo/Gyfu X
Deities Saturn, Dionysus/Bacchus, the Dark Goddess
Other associations The elements of Earth and Water, elves, love, wisdom, light, purification, dignity.

Dutch elm disease destroyed many of the mature elms in Britain. The elm used to be one of the tallest trees in the British Isles, reaching heights of 45 metres (150 feet) after 100 years of growth, and living to 400. Elm is associated with purification and is astringent and anti-inflammatory. The cleansing qualities of elm also act upon the spirit, helping us to be rid of depression, inadequacy and anything that hinders the growth of our spirit. Elm is also used in incense for the same purpose. Elm is used for furniture, although if not well-seasoned it warps easily. It is also used for coffins.

Like many trees, stories link the elm with Orpheus. Greek legend tells how the first elm-grove sprang up to the poignant strains of Orpheus, on his return from the Underworld, playing a lament for the loss of his lady Eurydice. An old Italian tradition encourages a connection between the elm and the vine, planting them together so that the

former can provide shade and a growing frame for the latter. Elms are also linked to the elven folk, who guard burial mounds and who were believed to guard against lightning and to help in the attraction of love. Elm trees were called 'elven'. Elves had contact with the ancestors and so kings could receive good counsel from approaching them. Like the elves, elm has a sombre and a light side, for justice was dispensed beneath its branches, while elm can be carried to attract love and luck. Perhaps the most exquisite and vivid portrait of elves is given by Tolkien in *Lord of the Rings* – eternally youthful, inexpressibly wise, unutterably ancient, wistful, heroic, beautiful and magical. The time of these beings in Middle Earth was coming to an end – as the time for elms has come to an end, temporarily, at least – and they were slowly departing over the Great Sea, while terrible danger threatened the world. How striking a metaphor for our times! Elm is a connection to older, wiser, times and while it is associated with death, it is also a passage to that dimension where nothing dies.

GHOST GUM

Eucalyptus papuana
Deities   Eucalyptus may be associated with the Moon and Saturn
Other associations   The element of Water, healing.

This is another Australian eucalypt, called *papuana* because it is indigenous to Papua. The ghost gum appears in most parts of Australia north of the Tropic of Capricorn, preferring sandy soil and often found in rocky places. It reaches between 9 and 20 metres (30 and 65 feet) in height. Its timber has been used for various purposes, rather from lack of anything better than from choice, for the wood isn't very hard and is not resistant to the termites that flourish in regions where it grows.

Ghost gums became widely known through the paintings of Rex Battarbee in the 1950s and his most famous Aboriginal pupil, Albert Namatjira.

This striking tree, with its eerie appearance, due to its smooth, pale bark sprinkled with powdery white dust, is one of Australia's most photographed trees. Natives use the dust to whiten their headbands.

Many of the eucalypts, including ghost gums and coolibahs were valued for the medicinal properties of their *kino*, or astringent inner bark. These were used by Aboriginals and settlers alike, dissolved and gargled for sore throats, bathed on to sores and swallowed for diarrhoea. Kinos are rich in tannins that promote healing, and ghost gums especially were used to heal wounds.

A simple healing spell can be performed by rubbing eucalyptus oil on to a candle and burning it, visualising the person as totally well (do not visualise the disease disappearing, just complete health). Alternatively, surround your candle with eucalyptus leaves as it burns.

maple

Acer campestre
Rune Man/Mannaz ᛗ ᛉ
Deity Jupiter
Other associations The maple leaf is the emblem of Canada. Element of air, lovers, longevity.

The sap of maple can be made into delicious syrup and wine. Wassail bowls were made of maple and children were passed through the branches of this tree so they would enjoy a long life. This timber lends itself well to carving.

The tree we call sycamore is actually a type of maple – *Acer pseudoplatanus* – the true sycamore being a type of fig. Sycamore seeds have wings or 'keys' making them aerodynamic and a good choice to be placed on the altar for rituals linked to the element of Air, to swift thought and insight and when we seek the 'key' to wisdom.

Here is a seventeenth century wassail recipe, given by Yvonne Aburrow in *The Enchanted Forest* (see Further Reading).

> *Boil three pints of ale; beat six eggs the whites and yolks together, set both to the fire in a pewter pot; add roasted apples, honey, beaten nutmegs, clover and ginger; and being well-brewed drink it hot.*

The eggs may be left out and cider used instead of beer – guaranteed to warm the coldest winter's evening!

PINE

Pinus sylvestris
Ogham   Ailm
Rune   Kano/Ken   〈 ᚺ ᛉ

Deities   Mars, Freyr, Osiris, Cybele, Dionysus/Bacchus
Other associations   Birth, foresight, purification, the element of Air (and possibly Fire), incense.

Conifers are the most ancient of plants, for they flourished in the primeval forest, after the glacial period and before the appearance of the broadleaved trees. Pine can grow to 30 metres (98 feet) and reach an age of 600 years. Pine has properties that are beneficial to chest complaints when used as an inhalant. It is also good for cystitis, as an expectorant, stimulant, tonic and antiseptic. Pine is widely used for furniture, acquiring an attractive, honey tone. The presence of pine gives a realistic boost to confidence, it is exhilarating and cleansing enabling us to leave behind our mistakes and proceed with clarity and due humility. Used as an incense it is good for getting rid of negativity, for exorcism, protection, healing and defence.

One version of Greek legend tells how the goddess Cybele, who was worshipped in orgiastic cults similar to those of the wine god Dionysus, was loved by Attis, a handsome shepherd. When he proved unfaithful to her she changed him into a pine tree, but she regretted this so Zeus, her son, decreed that the pine would never lose its needles, staying green throughout the year as a consolation for her loss. Attis is one of many forms of the dying and resurrecting god of nature, who is, in fact, much older than the Corn King. The resurrecting god precedes the discovery of agriculture and reaches back to the time of the hunter-gatherers and herding peoples. The symbolism contained herein and the great height of pine give it the quality of foresight and indeed sight in all directions. A most ancient tree, Scots pine is the only tree from northern Europe to have survived the Ice Age. However, the old pine forests are a thing of the past, and current plantations are not always pleasant to walk in, for they have a synthetic aura that cramps the life of the trees – they are to the ancient forests what a modern block of flats is to a Gothic

79

cathedral. Clumps of Scots pine are believed to have been used as ley-line markers, where the potent currents of earth-energy flowed. Pine is a reminder of our heritage and a pointer to our future.

poplar and aspen

Populus – Salicaceae family
Rune Eolh/Eihwaz ↑
Deities Saturn, Hades/Pluto, Hecate, Persephone, Mercury, Demeter
Other associations The elements of Water, Earth and Air, eloquence, psychism, cycles of time, protection from illness.

Poplars prefer low-lying, moist areas, where rivers run. Black and white poplars grow to 30 metres (98 feet), the aspen grows more slowly and is a graceful tree, reaching 21 metres (69 feet) and beginning to decay internally after about fifty years. Aspen leaves tremble at the slightest breeze. White poplar has a silvery trunk while black poplar has bark that is almost black. The wood is light and has few uses, although the grey poplar – a cross between the white and black poplars – is harder and has a variety of uses. Being light and buoyant, poplar was used for oars and shields. Poplars have the ability to shield on many levels, acting as wind-breaks when planted in a line and, more subtly, poplar drives out fear. The presence of poplar is reassuring and grounding, enabling delusion to be left behind.

Aspen is especially connected to Mercury – the god who could travel in and out of the Underworld – and the wearer of an aspen crown could visit the Underworld and return. Aspen has been found in burial mounds dating from 3000BCE. Aspen vibrates to the gentlest breath of wind, as if it hears whispers from afar. It is connected to the Maiden aspect of the Triple Goddess, of whom Persephone is an example. Persephone was the beloved daughter of the earth goddess, Demeter, who was abducted by Pluto, King of the Underworld. Everything withered as Demeter mourned her daughter, so the gods bargained that Persephone should return for eight months of the year to her mother and go down below for four, to be with the dark

lord as his queen (this myth varies in respect of the months accorded – the Greek winter is shorter than the British!). We may assume that Persephone secretly chooses her 'fate' as an initiation and a passage to power. This is one tale of how the seasonal cycle was established. White poplar we may link with the Mother aspect of the Triple Goddess, represented by Demeter. Black poplar is Hecate's tree – associated with the Crone. Black poplar 'weeps' with sticky balsam, because the sisters of Phaethon were turned into poplars by the gods who pitied their mourning for their brother. Phaethon, son of Helios the sun god, begged to be allowed to drive the brilliant chariot of the sun, but he could not control the mighty horses and, flying too near the earth, he parched it. Whereupon Zeus, king of the gods, fell into a rage and slew him with a thunderbolt in full view of his horrified sisters. However, what dies is also, someday, reborn. Hecate, goddess of witches, teaches us not to fear the darkness but to go through it and be transformed. Poplars in the three aspects mentioned are connected to the lunar cycle, waxing, full and waning and it is probably from the disappearance and reappearance of the moon that humans first learnt to have faith that what goes also comes back. All trees teach us about cyclicity, none more clearly than poplar.

sequoia

Family *Taxodiaceae – Sequoia sempervirens* (Coast Redwood); *Sequoiadendron gigantum* (Wellingtonia) and *Metasequoia glyptostroboides* (Dawn Redwood)

The Redwood is native to the Pacific Coast of North America and the Wellingtonia to the Sierra Nevada mountains of California. The Dawn Redwood was at one time known only as a fossil and was 'discovered' in China in 1941. These trees are related to the pine family and are among the world's largest and oldest living creatures. Coast Redwoods are the world's tallest trees, often growing to a height of 90 metres (295 feet), taking about 2,000 years to reach this immensity. However, the giant sequoia may be even older. The oldest, called General Sherman, grows in the Sequoia National Park in California and is believed to be between 3,000 and 4,000 years old. It is 83 metres (272 feet) tall and has a diameter of more then 9 metres (30 feet). Giant sequoias grow mostly in groves protected by the US government. The tallest British sequoia grows at Endersleigh in Devon and is bout 50 metres (164 feet) in height. Both trees produce small cones and timber that is light but strong and durable.

These majestic trees have become to some extent synonymous with the pride and endurance of Nature and with all that is worth preserving in native culture and attitudes. Their names comes from the North American leader and inventor of the Cherokee alphabet, Sequoya. His name may also be spelt Sequoyah or Sequoia. Probably the son of a Cherokee woman and an English trader, he is also remembered by his English name George Guess. Sequoya was determined to preserve the culture of the Cherokees and he developed a system of writing for them, in an alphabet of more than eighty characters that contained all the syllables of the Cherokee language. Thus newspapers and books could be produced for them and thousands learned to read and write this new written communication. Here we have another link between trees and the transmission and organisation of information for humanity.

5

FORESTS – OUR PAST AND OUR FUTURE

I think that I shall never see
A billboard lovely as a tree
Perhaps unless the billboards fall
I'll never see a tree at all

Ogden Nash, *Song of the Open Road*

Those who work and live close to the land are rarely sentimental about Nature, knowing that life depends on death. Many passages in this book comment on the uses of wood and other tree-products. It is not possible to stop cutting down trees. However, it is absolutely vital that we rethink what we are doing to trees and proceed with common sense and respect for the dignity, beauty and value of their life forms. There are many environmental problems that currently beset us, but deforestation may, arguably, be the most serious. John Fowles, in *The Rising Sun handbook* says:

It is not Christ who is crucified now, it is the tree itself, and on the bitter gallows of human greed and stupidity. Only suicidal morons, in a world already choking to death, would destroy the best natural air conditioner creation affords.

Not all the dangers of cutting down forests are immediate or obvious. Species are becoming extinct at a rate of over 20,000 per year, but what is also being lost is the habitat and the opportunity for nature to evolve new forms as a replacement. Bacteria which inhabit forest depths are being released into the atmosphere, and where the forest might have contained them, that environment is being destroyed. Forests are disappearing at a crazy rate – in the Brazilian Amazon alone an area approximately the size of Belgium has been lost in the last five years. Many areas turn to desert once the forests are gone and these losses will take nature millions of years to repair. Only 6 per cent of remaining forests are protected – well below the desirable minimum of 10 per cent and even those may not be effectively so. While we self-righteously lament the loss of rainforests, destruction forges ahead in our own country, sacrificing trees to make roads, build houses or lay cables for television.

Humanity started life in the forests, swinging from branch to branch to avoid predators. On the scale of evolution that is not so long ago. Tiny babies are born with a grip so strong it will support their weight, conditioned to grip mother's fur or neck and later on to swing through the trees by themselves. Trees have long been our friends, guardians and givers of life to the hunter-gatherer peoples. Environmentalists keep stating facts about the importance of trees and idealists fight for them, but there is also a feeling of despair among nature-lovers – what can one possibly say that has not been said? Respect for nature has become a cliché – something that characterises New Age softies, while those in power behave as if they were the ones with common sense, patronising and marginalising the protestors. Humanity is like an egotistic adolescent, adopting that bored look in the face of adult advice. It is neither 'adult' nor sensible to keep on developing – when are we going to wake up? Richard Nixon said 'When you've seen one redwood you've seen them all' and that epitomises the general attitude. Those who do care often retreat, hopeless and impotent, finding it too painful to witness the destruction. In the words of a

native American 'Only when the last tree has been felled will people wake up to the fact that you can't eat money'.

STANDING UP FOR TREES

Protest on behalf of trees cannot be wasted, however. Even when it seems that nothing has been accomplished and the last proud tree falls to make way for yet another bypass, if even one more person has come alive to the importance of trees as a result of a protest made, then it has been worthwhile. We must go on protesting, because it is the only way. Each of us can do what we can. Recently it seemed our local wood was under threat. I don't have the time – or, frankly, the guts, to chain myself to a tree, but I heard of a local adolescent who was prepared to do so and I promised that I would bring her hot soup! Luckily the threat receded, for the time being. Effective protest is not necessarily successful protest, for publicity is valuable. Here are a few pointers to making your view count.

- Get well informed. The rainforests are a long way away and there will be plenty happening in your own neck of the woods. Go down to the local planning authority's offices and find out what developments are planned. Will they threaten trees or other valuable sites?
- Get into groups, even small ones are better than solitary work, for some people have more time than others and tasks can be apportioned – everyone can be encouraged to lend a hand when they might feel what they could offer on their own was too insignificant to bother with.
- Resist the temptation to break the law, in any way, or even to act in an anti-social manner. Your feelings of desperation and aggression are quite understandable, but don't give in to them. It simply will not advance your cause. In fact it will harm it. Remember *you* are the voice of sanity.
- Publicity is your greatest asset. Interest local and national press. Get a celebrity in to help you. Anything that isn't harmful or stupid that can grab the headlines is good, good, good.

- Don't be put off if you can't do very much – just do a little bit, and do what you feel able. Good at letter-writing? Then do that. Offer what you can.
- Don't be put off by failure – it's almost inevitable at the moment, but the voice of the conservationists is getting louder.
- For your own part, avoid buying over-packaged goods that use paper unnecessarily, use recycled paper and recycle your old paper products. And plant a tree – it is a really positive act.

Hug a tree

Yet another New Age cliché, but trees have long been known for their healing properties. You don't have to have physical contact with a tree, but just being inside the aura of the tree is beneficial. Trees can help with health in so many ways. In fact, they can be a barometer to the health of the area, for most trees are affected by pollution and geopathic stress. An area where the trees grow strong and healthy is probably a safe place for humans.

Practice – using trees in rituals

At the end of the first chapter you will have found some suggestions for creating a tree ceremony. The sort of ceremony envisioned was one that centred, to a large extent, on the tree; but what about using trees in smaller rituals, possibly private ones, when we have a specific goal in mind? Some suggestions for magical use of trees are found in the chapter 'Trees and Magic' but you can incorporate trees into your rituals in many ways, starting with a list of basic correspondences.

The most obvious use of tree-essence is in incense and again examples of blends are given in the earlier chapter. Wood is also notably used to fashion wands – use your knowledge of and feelings about the tree to determine your choice. Wood is a

valuable substance in magical rites and some traditions exclude the use of anything metal from their rituals. This presumably originates from the time before the Iron Age, possibly even the Bronze Age, identifying the most ancient practices as the most magical. Thus a staff might be used to describe the circle instead of the sword favoured by some traditions and the wand used instead of the athame (symbolic knife) although athames of flint or other stone can be acquired. Tree products can be used in other ways in rituals, simply by placing leaves, twigs, nuts, fruit and blossom on the altar or by consecrating a decoction of a relevant tree, instead of wine, in a ritual. Naturally care must be taken that poisonous species are not used. An acorn could be dedicated as a love or luck charm, dried leaves burnt as a 'letting go, moving on' ritual, etc. You can use your imagination.

Below is a list of basic correspondences that will give pointers to the use of trees in ritual. Under each of the trees listed, both in the birth trees chapter and the selection, you will find mention of associated deities and among these there will be one of the planets, the sun or moon. (Sun may appear as 'solar deities' and where much mention is made of goddess aspects, the moon may be appropriate, Maiden for Waxing, Mother for Full, Crone for Waning.) These planetary associations form the basis for the following correspondences. However, as you will have noticed from the information given, the symbolism of trees is very complex and may seem superficially contradictory, so always go essentially by what you feel. In addition, Uranus, Neptune and Pluto, the more recently discovered planets, are not included in this old system. Uranus is associated with change, revelation, inspiration, the intuitive flash, themes of innovation and new perspectives (hazel springs to mind here). Generally Uranus can be linked to the rulership of Mercury and sometimes the sun. Neptune is about dreams, ideals, contact with the Divine and the unseen realms. This may link with Moon and Venus rulerships. Pluto is about deep transformation, evolution, renewal and this may also be associated with the Moon, especially Waning and Dark, also sometimes with Saturn and often with Mars.

As an example of combining ideas for magical use, beech is ruled by Saturn, used in the treatment of skin complaints and connected with writing. To strengthen our psychic 'skin' for protection, self-containment or whatever, beech wood might be our choice and we might scratch some appropriate words or signs on a beech twig to carry with us, bury or burn, as we felt appropriate.

LIST OF CORRESPONDENCES

Sun   Health, protection, legal matters, enlightenment, success and energy in the magical and physical. Orange or gold. Leo. Lion, cats. Amber, carnelian, diamond, tiger's eye, sunstone. Tarot card The Sun. Sunday.

Moon   Home, fertility, family, healing, gardening, dreams, spirituality, love. White and silver (black may be waning or dark, and red for Full). Cancer. Fish, dolphins, snake, dog, bear. Aquamarine, chalcedony, quartz, moonstone, mother-of-pearl. Tarot card The High Priestess. Monday.

Mercury   Intelligence, eloquence, study, communication, travel, divination, wisdom. Yellow. Gemini and Virgo. Monkeys, swallows. Agate, aventurine, mottled jasper. Tarot card The Magician. Wednesday.

Venus   Love, beauty, youth, joy, happiness, reconciliation, pleasure, friendship, compassion, mediation. Blue and pink/rose. Taurus and Libra. Doves, swans. Emerald, lapis-lazuli, turquoise. Tarot card The Empress. Friday.

Mars   Courage, assertion, healing (after surgery), strength, sexuality, defence, exorcism. Red. Aries and Scorpio. Rams, scorpions, horses. Bloodstone, flint, red jasper, garnet, ruby. Tarot card The Tower. Thursday.

Jupiter   Prosperity, legal settlements, spiritual and religious matters, psychism and meditation. Purple. Pisces and Sagittarius. Centaur, horse, eagle. Amethysts, lepidolite. Tarot card Wheel of Fortune. Tuesday.

Saturn   Binding, grounding, centring, protecting, purifying, certain kinds of luck, fertilising, nurturing, ending, preserving. Black, grey, dark green, dark brown. Capricorn and Aquarius. Goats and horned animals. Apache tear, jet, onyx, obsidian. Tarot card The World. Saturday.

FURTHER READING AND RESOURCES

Book and magazines

Tree Wisdom by Jacqueline Memory Paterson, Thorsons, 1996. An invaluable in-depth guide – most inspirational.

The Enchanted Forest by Yvonne Aburrow, Capall Bann, 1993. Comprehensive and full of information about magic, symbology and craft uses.

I am especially indebted to the above two volumes for information in completing this book.

The Druid Tradition by Philip Carr-Gomm, Element, 1991. Good basic guide to Druidry.

Myths of the Sacred Tree by Moyra Caldecott, Destiny, 1993. Many myths concerning trees, beautifully recounted.

Year of Moons, Season of Trees by Pattalee Glass-Koentop, Llewellyn, 1991. Celtic tree magic, celebrations and rites.

The Handbook of Celtic Astrology by Helena Paterson, Llewellyn, 1995. An interesting reference for the thirteen-sign lunar zodiac.

Secret Places of the Goddess by Philip Heselton, Capall Bann, 1995. A lovely companion to those seeking the Earth Spirit.

Witchcraft – A Beginner's Guide by Teresa Moorey, Hodder & Stoughton, 1996. An introduction to the Craft with explanations about ritual, correspondences, etc.

Paganism – A Beginner's Guide; *Herbs for Magic and Ritual – A Beginner's Guide*; *The Goddess – A Beginner's Guide*; by Teresa Moorey and *Pagan Gods for Today's Man – A Beginner's Guide* by Howard and Teresa Moorey. The last two are useful for expanding

some of the mythology in this book. All published by Hodder
& Stoughton.

The Wheel of the Year – Myth and Magic Through the Seasons by
Teresa Moorey and Jane Brideson, Hodder & Stoughton, 1996.
Explanation of the eight festivals and various ways of tuning in to
them, mythologically, practically and psychologically.

The Magical Lore of Herbs by Marion Davies, Capall Bann, 1994.
Tracing the use of plants through the ages, with sections on the
festivals and the magic of trees.

Cunningham's Encyclopaedia of Magical Herbs by Scott
Cunningham, Llewellyn, 1994. Contains references to trees and
extensive tables of correspondences.

Trees by Allen J. Coombes, Eyewitness Handbooks, Dorling
Kindersley, 1992; and

Trees of Britain and Europe by Bob Press and David Hosking, New
Holland, 1993. Two excellent pictorial guides.

Roger Oxley Looks at Australian Trees, Roger Oxley, ABC Books, 1993.

Caduceus Magazine, Issue 35, Spring 1997. This issue has much tree
information. Address: 38 Russell Terrace, Leamington Spa, Warks.
CV31 1HE, UK, e-mail: caduceus@oryx.demon.co.uk

Useful addresses

United Kingdom

Alarm UK (Against road-building; information pack and newsletter.)
13 Stockwell Road
London SW9 9AU

Friends of the Earth
26–28 Underwood Street
London N1 7JQ

Dragon (Eco-pagan action group.)
39 Amersham Road
London SE14 6QQ

International Tree Foundation
Sandy Lane
Crawley Down '
West Sussex RH10 4HS

Pagan Federation
BM BOX 7097
London WC1N 3XX

Canada

Hecate's Loom (Pagan magazine)
Box 5206
Station B
Victoria BC V8R 6N4

USA

Green Egg Magazine (Eco-paganism)
Box 1542
Ukiah
CA 95482

Australia

Church of all Worlds
PO Box 408
Woden ACT 2606

Pagan Ozzies can contact:

John and Chel Bardell
Administrators of the Australian Pagan Alliance
P O Box 823
Bathurst
NSW 2795
Australia